TODAY
and Yesterday

TODAY
and Yesterday

John Timpson

London
George Allen & Unwin Ltd
Ruskin House   Museum Street

© George Allen & Unwin (Publishers) Ltd, 1976
ISBN 0 04 927008 7

Printed in Great Britain
in 11 point Baskerville type
by Willmer Brothers Limited, Birkenhead

To the 'Today' team – especially Pat,
for whom the alarm clock bell also tolls

Chapter One

They were very civil about it, but the message was perfectly clear.

'Timpson,' they said, 'it would appear that you are not learning anything from us – and we are certainly not learning anything from you.'

So ended, rather prematurely, four convivial but largely unproductive years at Merchant Taylors' School.

Such was the system of specialisation in those days that from the age of twelve, thanks to an early aptitude for adding up cricket scores in my head, I had been labelled a scientist and mathematician. Much of my school life had therefore been spent in a bewildering world of test-tubes and prisms and electrical circuits, keeping an eye on my more talented neighbours to see what happened to their experiments and ensuring that one way or another, mine turned out the same. By such devices I achieved matriculation, but there is a limit to bluff, even in science. As the work became more complex, so the co-ordinate geometry became less co-ordinated, the calculus became more incalculable. By the end of the Easter term of 1945, when I was still sixteen, we mutually agreed to call it a day.

But what path to take now? Certainly not to the laboratories, nor to a City office. My father had caught the 8.10 to a Trafalgar Square bank for as long as I could remember; it was worthy work and he enjoyed it, but it held no appeal for me. Only two paths seemed at all attractive. Neither appeared to require much effort (which of course was part of the attraction) and certainly neither involved the BBC. One led to the London Palladium, the other to Fleet Street.

I had been playing about in amateur dramatics since my dancing teacher first dressed me in a sailor suit and pushed me onto the stage to execute a solo hornpipe. I was four at the time, and when the curtain rose I fled sobbing to the wings. But when the show was over and the doting relatives flocked round, it was not the hard-working tap-dancers or the talented little ballet girls who attracted the attention, it was that sweet little chap in the sailor suit who had looked such a poppet when his eyes filled with tears. So I learned my first lesson in audience reaction: it is not necessarily the item which has involved the most work that people remember, it is the one which is different, preferably the one that goes wrong. It applied to dancing displays then, and it applies now to 'Today'.

The first public appearance – 'The Sailor's Hornpipe' in a dancing display. Alas, I was not so blithe in the actual display; as the curtain rose, I fled, weeping, from the stage.

That first flicker of the limelight was so enjoyable that in the years that followed I sought more. My mother, as well as apparently running every whist drive and sale of work in the northern Home Counties, also belonged to an assortment of amateur dramatic societies; almost nightly, it seemed, she was to be seen playing anything from a comic grandma or an aged retainer to Lady Macbeth. With this entrée into the local Thespian scene, and thanks to the natural reluctance of most young lads to make fools of themselves in public, I had a fairly clear field among the juvenile leads. The local church youth club even tolerated my efforts as an impresario, and luckless friends and relations were regaled twice a year with revues entitled, for instance, 'The Follies of Youth' – devised by, written by, produced by, and starring . . . It was great for the ego, but a little wearing, I suspect, for the friends and relations.

With all this theatrical background, plus two school elocution prizes and an ability to fall heavily without injuring myself (thanks to a recent performance as the doomed Duke of Clarence en route for the butt of malmsey), my destiny seemed clear. My parents, however, tolerant though they were of my scholastic shortcomings, and resigned to my decision not to catch the 8.10 to Trafalgar Square, did at last draw the line. The stage at any time, and certainly during the war, offered a degree of insecurity comparable only to going over Niagara in a barrel. Surely, they said wearily, you could try something else. The Palladium shut its doors, and Fleet Street began to beckon.

I had been putting typewriter keys to paper ever since my mother bought a machine for her numerous voluntary secretarial duties, found she could not quite get the hang of it, and asked me to type her minutes instead. Thus, incidentally, I acquired an intimate knowledge of the inner workings of the Townswomen's Guild movement which has stood me in good stead ever since. By the time I was fifteen I was producing a form magazine (frequently suppressed), writing appalling short stories and unperformable plays, and generally feeling no end of a literary dog. The words seemed to come easily and people occasionally smiled sympathetically when they read them. This, I felt must be where the future lay. Better still, could I not combine the two professions, and find a job where I could write and then perform what I had written? There was such a job, but Noel Coward had already got it. I did not realise at the time that in their own way the great radio correspondents of the day were also combining these two talents, except that they dealt in facts instead of fiction. Nor could I know that in due course the same combination would be required, on a more modest scale, from presenters of 'Today'.

The merits of journalism as a career seemed considerable, particularly to anyone as basically idle as me. It apparently required no academic qualifications, it involved no set working hours, and it had that faint aura of romance and drama which Philip Gibbs did so much to foster in his *Street of Adventure*. It was a world of green eyeshades and follow-that-cab and hold-the-front-page; above all, it did not involve getting up early in the morning. In short, it seemed worth a try, but how to start? Even if Merchant Taylors' had boasted a career advisory service in those days, one career it would have been unlikely to advise on with any enthusiasm was journalism. Most of my school friends were heading for university or the Services or the boardrooms of their fathers' companies. One or two masters may have contributed an occasional letter to *The Times*, but their view of the yellow Press was, appropriately, jaundiced.

The school had produced a Clive of India and a Gilbert Murray and even a Titus Oates, but it was pretty thin on Frank Owens and Arthur Christiansens. It was only years later that I found how close I had been to the whiff of printer's ink: a gangling, prematurely bald lad in my year called Tony Thompson was later to blossom in the quality Sundays using his mother's maiden name and signing himself Anthony Lejeune.

If the school was no help, there were even fewer contacts at home. Not many star Fleet Street reporters could be found whooping it up in The Ridgeway, Kenton, a neat and quiet street lined with neat quiet semis occupied by neat and quiet people. It was another thirty years before a Ridgeway resident achieved national glory, when the notable Liberal, Desmond Banks, a one-time performer in those church youth club revues, received a life peerage and took the title of Baron Banks of Kenton. I like to think he may have originally thought of that title for one of our Christmas pantomimes – how splendid that he should take it to the House of Lords.

My own family could offer no guidance on launching a journalistic career. Had I needed advice on interest rates or deposit accounts my father could have supplied it in abundance. Had I wanted to cook a dinner for twelve while simultaneously making a stair carpet, teaching a first-aid class and playing a hand of bridge, my mother could have provided all the tips. Had I even wanted to play the bassoon, thus continuing the family's musical tradition (my parents had first met in an amateur orchestra, father playing the piano, mother the violin), I would have had every encouragement and help. As it happened, my sister Joy inherited all the musical talent, and earned a string of letters to become eventually a senior professor of music at a teachers' training college. After years of agonising piano lessons I could play only a few simple melodies from *The Dancing Years* – musical comedy seemed another possibility at one time – and the bottom line of Liszt's 'Hungarian Rhapsody.' The top line, which was much more difficult, used to be played by Basil Banks, brother of the Baron-to-be, in a comedy duo act which involved, as I recall, falling off the piano stool when I reached the very low notes. Here again the good old Duke of Clarence had provided invaluable experience.

All of this offered little ammunition for storming the Fleet Street barricades. I discovered that there were two recognised methods of attack: one was through the universities, which provided most of the leader writers and specialist correspondents; the other was through the local Press, the training ground for the general reporter. In 1945 I could find no schools of journalism, no courses to be studied or diplomas to be won. Somehow the profession struggled along without them and one learned as one went along.

The first move was to enrol in a shorthand class at Harrow Technical College. There were about thirty girl students, training as secretaries, and me. Amazingly, I did actually learn a little shorthand. At the same time I started knocking on editors' doors. The *Harrow Observer* had no vacancies. The *Wembley Observer* turned out to be a sister paper of the Harrow one, and they had no vacancies either. The third call was at their rival's. the *Wembley News*, later to be absorbed by the Observer group, but at that time independently owned, with a healthy circulation and even a sister paper called the *Kingsbury & Kenton News* (exactly the same as the Wembley version except for the masthead, but they were not to know that in Kingsbury and Kenton). I had ten minutes with the editor, ostentatiously sporting my OMT tie (which he didn't recognise) and lying about my shorthand speed. I emerged a Gentleman of the Press, on a month's trial at thirty shillings a week plus bicycle allowance.

As in most local newspaper offices in those closing months of the war, nearly all the regular staff were away in the Forces. The owner of the paper, Mervyn Harley, was officially the editor, and indeed he did keep a fatherly eye on us and curtailed our wilder exploits, but he had other interests as well and most weeks the paper was brought out by the four reporters, all of us still in our teens. David Lalor, invalided out of the Navy soon after joining it, was editor of the film page, which meant that he wrote the reviews from the film company handouts, had first look at the *Kine Weekly* und was in charge of the free passes to the local cinemas. Brian Robins, ardent Liberal canvasser, was at eighteen our expert on local government, not only because of his political aspirations (he was later to become an alderman) but also because he was the only one of us whose shorthand could keep up with council debates. Gerald Whiting was our church correspondent, devoting much of his time to reversing tradition by visiting the local clergy and taking tea with them. In view of my Thespian background I was made drama critic and (more obscurely) compiler of the women's page. We shared out the wedding reports, court cases and annual dinners, and anyone at a loose end did the sport.

My first job was the obituaries, which did not involve any great literary talent. All I had to do was visit the three local undertakers who advertised with us, collect the names of their clients, and list them under the simple valediction, 'The *News* regrets to record the deaths of the following local residents . . .' If there were any local undertakers who had the bad taste not to advertise with us, then I fear their customers were despatched without The *News* recording any regrets at all.

Wedding reports came in on our standard forms, to which we tried to impart a few touches of individuality by juggling the order of the answers. 'At St Michael's Church, Tokyngton, on Saturday . . .' we would start one report. 'Wearing a full-length dress of white satin and tulle . . .' would start the next. 'Given away by her father . . .' started the third. Eventually the introductions became so convoluted as to be unrecognisable to the couple concerned. 'Two young people whose parents belonged to Alperton Bowls Club before the war . . .' or 'Music for dancing was supplied by the Preston Road Five at the reception after the wedding of . . .' and once even 'Walking with the aid of a stick as the result of an accident at work in which a heavy packing case fell on his foot, breaking two toes and severely bruising his ankle, Mr X was one of the guests at the wedding of . . .'

Most court cases fell into standard patterns too, which was just

6

as well. This was long before the NUJ Proficiency Training Scheme, through which juniors learn about court procedure before actually being let loose in court, and many a time we must have risked charges of contempt or libel as we tried to set out an hour of legal wrangling in a few lines of simple print. The invaluable word 'alleged' became etched on our typewriters: 'It was alleged that the defendant had driven at an alleged speed of 45 miles an hour in an alleged built-up area after allegedly ignoring an alleged red light.' But with two mornings a week at Wealdstone Court, another two mornings at Hendon, and juvenile court on alternate Wednesdays, we gradually grasped why some cases were committed for trial while others were dealt with summarily, why some evidence was admissible while another kind was not, why some charges were pressed while others were dropped and, most important of all, why some facts could be reported while others could not.

Along with the speeding cases and the drunks, the shoplifters and the defrauders of London Transport, there were also the occasional embezzlers, the burglars (not to be confused, we learned, with housebreakers), the wife-beaters and the rapists. For a seventeen-year-old, it was a useful grounding in the ways of the world as well as the ways of the law.

Drama criticism could be even trickier than court reporting. No amateur actor, as I well know, enjoys being told how bad he is. He buys his local paper to see his name in print, preferably spelt correctly, and to read how bad all the others were. But now I had crossed the footlights and entered the Fifth Estate, as newly appointed guardian of the public weal and inheritor of the mantle of Bernard Shaw and James Agate, it was my obvious duty to tell it the way it was. After a succession of enraged letters to the editor, and the cancellation of several subscriptions, I resigned myself to telling it the way it nearly was.

I still felt that if amateurs were prepared to take the public's money at the box office they should take criticism as well, though perhaps not, I eventually admitted, from a seventeen-year-old, no matter how many Follies of Youth he may have perpetrated in his own church hall. As I gained experience both as a performer and as a critic I still tried to temper justice with mercy. No matter how thick-skinned even a professional performer becomes, there is something about the printed attack on one's talents and ability which, however, justified, can still make the stomach turn.

7

As a spin-off from my dramatic criticisms I was occasionally detailed to act as music critic too. Here I floundered in unknown waters, where it was much easier to suppress any critical conscience and juggle with a cowardly assortment of 'delightfuls' and 'enchantings' and 'admirably executeds'. The performers themselves seemed well satisfied with this approach; only the shades of long-dead composers must have marvelled at such perfidy. Even on a local paper, though, one can become too blasé, and with one report of a concert at Wembley Town Hall I went too far. It had been even more appalling than usual, a series of items ranging from obnoxious boy sopranos to inexhaustible string quartets. At the interval I stole away, and in a nearby hostelry rewrote the programme with a liberal sprinkling of 'delightfuls' and 'admirably executeds'.

In a foolish moment of exuberance, however, I wrote of the final item: 'Miss G gave a memorable interpretation on the piano of Mendelssohn's Concerto in E.' It was only after the paper was on the streets that I learned how memorable that interpretation must have been, because Miss G, it appeared, had actually been performing on the violin. The editor was uninpressed by my explanation that I had been seated too near the back of the hall to detect the difference. The episode very nearly made me an ex-journalist before I was eighteen.

There were other, less orthodox duties to perform in those makeshift wartime days. Often on a Wednesday night, as press time approached and we still had eight columns to fill – the 'silly season' lasted most of the year at the *Wembley News* – we would sit in the office with a street map devising 'Rural Rambles Round Neasden,' or topping up the correspondence columns with 'Letters to the Editor' from imaginary troublemakers in West Hendon or creating a cookery feature out of a Ministry of Food circular. There was one Ministry recipe for a curiously named 'cut-and-come-again cake': a great stand-by, said the Ministry, and so indeed it was. It came again and again in the thin summer issues.

Then on Thursdays it was the Folder Rota. We Gentlemen of the Press took it in turns to forget our gentility and to sprawl beneath the elderly folding machine to count the papers into thirteens, that magic figure beloved of newspaper publishers and bakers. We emerged after four hours or so, begrimed with ink, aching and weary, but five bob the richer and who cared about

SOGAT and NATSOPA. Actually we had the happiest relations with our colleagues in the printing shop, none of whom wanted to sit under the folder anyway – they were earning far more than we were already. So they allowed us our little Thursday perk, and in return they kindly adjusted our grammar and our spelling for us in the way that printers do, to the considerable gratification of programmes like 'Today'.

Out of all those council meetings and court cases which we reported for the *Wembley News*, and even out of the flower shows and the fetes, there emerged for all of us an invaluable grounding in the craft of newspaper reporting. It taught us, for instance, the value of accuracy. On a national paper reporters live a long way from the people they write about, so inevitably they arrive in haste, they enquire in haste and they depart in haste again. It is not surprising that so often when the national press reports a story in which you are personally involved you find at least one error, in emphasis if not in fact. On a local paper, though, your readers are just around the corner. Make one mistake, and they will be inside the office. It need not be a big mistake – just a wrong initial, a name omitted from a committee, an incorrect date for the next church bazaar. Soon there will be desks being thumped and telephones being rung. This indeed is how it should be; since proper care over the right initial today can mean a libel action avoided tomorrow.

Similarly, if one can understand the workings of a borough council, in due course Parliament is easier to follow. Grasp the procedure at a magistrates' court, and the Old Bailey will lose its mystique. Above all we learned how to talk with people, and to persuade them to talk to us, and whether the chap you are interviewing is secretary of the local Trades Council or general secretary of the TUC, the basic principle is much the same. Often the people involved are much the same, too.

For eighteen months I laboured in the sparse journalistic vineyards adjoining the North-Circular Road. VJ-Day came and went, with the street parties and the services of thanksgiving, and in due course the interviews with the gaunt survivors of Changi Jail and the Burma Road. We saw little of the horrors of war on the *News*, but those haggard grey faces, the skeletal bodies, the misshapen limbs, brought home to us sophisticated, teenaged men of the world what war could really mean. I was unashamedly relieved that for me, the country's call came after the actual fighting was over.

It came, in fact, in October 1946. Brian had already left for the Air Force, where he tackled the unravelling of King's Regulations as efficiently as he had unravelled the minutes of Wembley Council. Gerry and I were called up together; he followed Brian into the lower echelons of the RAF, while my own destination was even humbler – the supply section of the Royal Army Service Corps. We bade our farewells, wrote an appreciation of each other in the *Wembley News* (mine said 'he showed an ability beyond his years', and I suspect that theirs did too), and vowed that the team would eventually be reunited. So indeed it was; we all returned in due course to the *News* and the little upstairs office, but the spirit of that formative period could never be revived and things were never quite the same again.

Chapter Two

Northern Ireland was not as traumatic in 1946 as it is today, but there must have been jollier places to spend one's first six weeks in the Army. We had journeyed northwards to Stranraer, taken the night ferry to Larne, and pursued a zig-zag route covering most of the Northern Irish railway system until we were delivered, still in civilian clothes but at heart already mutinous deserters, to Ballykinler Primary Training Centre, a cheerless establishment at the foot of the Mourne Mountains in County Down. During my six weeks there the Mountains of Mourne did not merely swape down to the sea, they washed down to it. The rain fell incessantly. Newly released from my mother's kindly apron strings and ever-active washtub, with laundrettes still a vision of the future, my clothes were either dirty and damp, or clean and very damp indeed. Vests and socks were rarely removed, since a woolly under-layer was just as vital by night as by day, to augment the ageing blankets.

A proper battledress uniform had yet to be earned, and we lived in dilapidated denims beneath enormous berets which sheltered us from the rain but provided little scope for elegance. Thus camouflaged we doubled hither and thither, in a permanent hurry to get nowhere in particular, and having got there we doubled back again. We studied the parts of the rifle, were advised of the horrors of venereal disease, and learned how to doze off while standing to attention without the thumbs wavering from the line of the seams of the trousers. They were making men of us, we gathered, and very dull it was too.

At odd weekends we were let loose in Belfast. For a shilling a night you could get a bed in the Salvation Army hostel, with an excellent egg-and-bacon breakfast for a few pence more. It may not have been the Europa, which I got to know so well twenty-five years later, but in many ways it was a lot more comfortable. At least in those days they had no need to frisk you as you went in, you could sit by a window without ducking every time a car backfired, and you could go to bed without the risk of being blasted out of it before morning. True, the rifles back at the camp had to be kept chained up in case the locals added them to their private armouries, but Belfast itself, while never exactly a swinging city, was on the surface at least a fairly civilised one. After the sodden frugality of Ballykinler it seemed the height of sophisticated good living.

I wish I could remember some of my companions of those dank days at the Primary Training Centre. We met as civilians, we parted as imitation soldiers, yet the process of conversion was so impersonal, and the denims and those ghastly berets made us all so anonymous, that it might have been easier to strike up a friendship between two tins of baked beans. We were taking more exercise and breathing more fresh air than most of us had experienced since we were in the Boy Scouts, and it left us little inclined to expend energy in the evenings on making merry or even making conversation. We were ships that passed in a long wet night, and I never met any of them again.

At the end of the six weeks we had not exactly been moulded into a lethal fighting machine, but we could stamp our boots and shout 'Hup-two-three, down-two-three' and swing our arms like anything. It was time to go through the specialised Army process of selecting square pegs for round holes. As it happened, I struck lucky. Since I was able to fill in the various forms in real joined-up writing, my literary leanings were immediately detected. Here is a man of education, they said, of sensitivity and mental acumen, and they sent me on a typing course in Cirencester. It turned out to be the most useful course I could have taken. Until then I had used the standard journalistic technique on a typewriter of two index fingers and a little brute force. For the next six weeks, with a wooden cover over the machine to conceal the keys, I learned to employ all eight fingers and both thumbs as we tapped out the saga of the quick brown fox jumping over the lazy dog, with the instructor thumping out the time like a Roman galley-master. My quick brown fox has been jumping fairly briskly ever since, and most useful it has been. I achieved my sixty words a minute and qualified for an S-oblique in front of my Army number: S/19078765-Sah. The S stood for Supply, and also for Soft Number, because when you are typing you cannot be drilling or latrine-cleaning or killing people.

Then they offered me a shorthand course, which no doubt would have been helpful too, but it lasted for nineteen weeks, which seemed an eternity, and they unwisely asked me instead of telling me. By now I knew that only an idiot volunteered for anything, so I resisted the one-pace-forward-*march*, and my name went into the hat for a posting.

In those days, and it probably still applies, an overseas posting was far preferable to staying in the UK, since the delights of being close to kith and kin were easily outweighed by the attractions of duty-free NAAFIS and currency fiddles and lording it over the natives. Even these attractions varied in degree: Hong Kong rated full marks, Malaya got a zero, while North Africa was too hot and Northern Europe too cold. Ideally you joined the garrison in Jamaica or showed the flag in the Seychelles, and I once met a happy soul who spent the entire war in Bermuda, keeping watch, as I understand it, for Japanese submarines. My posting turned out to be worth about seven out of ten in the ratings. BTA, they told me. I had to ask around quite a bit before anyone could tell me what it meant; I found I was to join the British Troops in Austria.

There were a lot of plusses about Austria. It was distant enough to be really abroad, but near enough to qualify for home leave every four or five months. The Austrians were comparatively friendly – at least they preferred us to the Germans – and the Austrian scenery was delightful. Into Alamein Transit Camp at Villach, where new drafts arrived from the UK, there floated all the curious flotsam of the BTA. Generally there were some four thousand men wandering about in the sort of aimless limbo that only the Army and airports can create. There were the disillusioned ones, travelling from unit to umpteenth unit and past caring why; the exultant ones, just going on leave, and the gloomy ones, just back; the drunks awaiting demobilisation; the 'college boys' just out of the military prison at nearby Lienz; and the furtive ones, absent without leave, who had found that the anonymity and confusion of a big transit camp can be a 'trotter's' paradise.

It was mid-winter when my draft was stirred into this strange gallimaufry, the kind of mid-winter that the real Alamein never knows. As our train pulled in after the two-day journey from Calais, I threw my kitbag onto the platform and it disappeared in three feet of snow. We skated rather than marched to the camp itself, stood in shivering misery for what seemed a day and a half until our billets were allocated, then found that the taps were frozen, the windows were iced up, and the fuel in the stoves produced not a smokeless heat but a special kind of heatless smoke. The cookhouse seemed to be somewhere the other side of Salzburg, the latrines seemed to straddle the Italian border. When you eventually located the NAAFI, midway between Zurich and Geneva, it was already packed to the doors and the beer had just run out. I therefore managed to contain my delight when they advised me that in view of my exceptional qualifications I was to stay on permanently at the camp as an orderly room clerk. The few acquaintances I had made on the journey were despatched to romantic Vienna, to lakeside Klagenfurt, up into the mountains at Graz. I was left in a deserted hut, surrounded by empty acres of trodden snow, with the feeling that somewhere I must have gone wrong.

But how differently a transit camp can appear when you are no longer just in transit. In practice a staff private had authority over any transitee, of whatever rank. To those who proved difficult he could allocate the draughtiest hut, the knobbliest mattress, the most sordid latrine. He held the meal tickets, the NAFFI tickets, the leave tickets; he made out the duty rosters, detailed the fatigue parties, and above all selected the postings. In fact I soon found the fellow who had assigned me to the staff – he had taken the list of S-obliques on my draft and picked me out with a pin. Thus is one's destiny determined in the Forces of the Crown.

I was two years on the staff of Alamein Camp, right through until my 'demob' number came up. They were two largely wasted years, but not entirely unenjoyable. I met some most entertaining people and made some very good friends, one of whom, Lance-Corporal Peter Bell (inevitably 'Clanger'), later acted as my best man and subsequently became my brother-in-law. We still keep in touch, too, with Basil Minson, a slow-speaking sergeant-clerk from Yeovil famous for the phrase, 'Oi'm larnin' graajully', with which he effectively silenced any officer who might unwisely reprimand him and which we all came to employ eventually in times of crisis.

It is the boredom which one remembers most. Many letters to *The Times* have been written, mostly by ex-officers, in praise of National Service and calling for its reintroduction to mould the flaccid characters of the sloppy young folk of today. It would provide discipline, they say, a change of scene, a chance to mingle with youngsters from different backgrounds and environments,

What the well-dressed National Serviceman was wearing to defend King and Country in 1946.

to learn to live together and tolerate one's fellow men. Much the same could be said about any well-run open prison.

Certainly we learned to tolerate our fellow men – if you did not tolerate them, then naturally they thumped you – and this was no bad thing. But since our only goal was to get the whole business

15

over with as little fuss and effort as possible, we also learned how to avoid responsibility or individual thought, to dodge every dodgeable column and to swing all available lead. The buck, as far as I could see, never stopped anywhere. The professional Army of today is no doubt very different, but if any characters were moulded by the conscript Army of the immediate post-war years, the final result must have been pretty bizarre. Life could be uncomfortable, occasionally downright unpleasant, but mostly it was a monumental bore.

In February 1949 I came home with a demob suit cut to fit Quasimodo, an evil-looking trilby which set Special Branch men searching their IRA folders, and one of those Army testimonials which made employers fall about. It did however include some fascinating tributes – not surprisingly, since I composed most of them. As well as the standard phrases about being honest, reliable and trustworthy, which applied to anyone who had not actually been convicted of armed robbery and even to some of those who had, I read of myself that 'in the sphere of journalism, his activities were particularly fruitful, and the newspaper he edited for the benefit of the soldiers passing through this camp was welcomed and read with lively interest. Signed M. Young, Captain RA, Adjutant.' I wonder if M. Young, Captain RA, Adjutant, remembers signing that rubbish one blurry morning, along with a sheaf of movement orders and leave passes? Does Captain Young remember at all the corporal 'of upright character, pleasing disposition and likeable personality, loyal and conscientious, extremely thorough in his work, capable of acting with initiative, nothing seems too much'? It is all there over his signature. I think I phrased it rather well.

However, when this paragon of military virtue showed up again at the *Wembley News*, prepared to take over the editorial chair – 'I have no hesitation in recommending this man for any position of responsibility which calls for sound organising and executive capabilities. Signed M. Young, Captain RA, Adjutant' – he found the situation very different from that he had left. The real editor had long since returned from the Services, experienced reporters were available again, unions were insisting on a proper quota of senior men in every office, even Brian and Gerry had returned ahead of me. I was back at the foot of the table again, a cub reporter with a lot of leeway to make up.

I like to think that the three of us held our own rather well against the much senior competition. The editor himself, Leslie Bland, a kindly and deeply conscientious man whose shorthand even after years of disuse in the Air Force still put ours to shame, gave us invaluable guidance which we had so lacked during those earlier years on our own. He is there still, and there must be dozens of young reporters who have cause to be grateful for his training and advice. I resumed my round of the courts and the councils, but now I could cope with the trickier cases and, I even followed the council minutes. I began to appreciate what errors I had fallen into, how much there was still to learn. In the next two years, I hope I learned it.

Life became a comfortable round of undemanding work among pleasant colleagues, with plenty of time for performing those amateur plays and living it up around the local church halls. I even had priority petrol coupons for my motor bike: reporting flower shows and jumble sales was classified as work of national importance, and no doubt rightly so. It was all rather pleasant really, and not being too energetic a fellow I would probably have been content to let it stay that way.

It was the motor bike that eventually broke the spell. It also broke my leg.

On my way to Hendon Court one morning, with a light rain falling and the roads very wet, a brick lorry emerged from a side road and in swerving I broadsided into it. My left knee was caught between the bike and the side of the lorry and has never really functioned properly since. For several weeks I was in hospital with my leg tied to the ceiling and a growing antipathy towards brick lorries but, like the random pin of that clerk who took me off the draft and posted me to the staff at Alamein, it proved a blessing in the end. It brought me the girl I married, and enough money in damages to marry her.

Pat was a nurse, and it would make a much better story if we had first met in hospital and she had nursed me back to health. In fact we had met some years before, when we both attended a church youth club harvest camp down in Wiltshire. She was cooking, I was harvesting. I recall that I actually harvested very little, since I spent most of the time in the kitchen, but it proved a very bountiful harvest in the end.

Since those days we had kept in touch but led our own lives, she among the medical fraternity at University College Hospital (my antipathy to brick lorries extends to medical students too), I among the more questionable delights of Austria. She completed her training as a staff nurse, qualified as a midwife, and was trailing six letters after her name by the time I was back at the *News*. We met at club dances and she sat through my shows, but it was the accident that brought things to a head. She visited me in hospital and pulled rank to get the curtains put round the bed.

The engagement photograph, July 1950. Out of the picture is the leg calliper which hampered the formal proposal.

She helped me with the crutches and the calliper that followed and in July 1950 we were engaged. It is no mean feat to go on one knee when the other is locked in a calliper, but I managed it. In fact I very nearly played 'We'll Gather Lilacs' with my free hand.

It seemed an appropriate time to get out of suburbia, but the industrial north did not attract me and Fleet Street was still out of reach. It would have to be a country community, far enough away from London to have a character of its own, not so far away that one vanished altogether. Not a commuter county like Sussex or Kent, not a holiday county like Dorset or Devon, but a place with its own way of life, somewhere a little different from everywhere else.

It turned out to be Norfolk.

It happened largely by chance, again like the posting clerk with the pin, for it was the first advertisement that I came across in the old *World's Press News*, the journalist's *Exchange & Mart*: 'District reporter wanted for the Norfolk News Company Ltd, serving local weekly as well as county morning and evening papers . . .' Came the application form, then the interview and the medical (they are careful whom they let into Norfolk), and in February 1951 I turned my back on the Harrow Road and the turrets of Wembley Stadium to join the Dereham office of the *Eastern Daily Press* and the *Eastern Evening News*. The office was also the headquarters of the *Dereham & Fakenham Times,* and very nearly, it seemed at the time, the edge of the civilised world.

Chapter Three

I had been to Norfolk only twice before. Once was on a family holiday to Cromer when it rained so heavily that the hotel basement had to be pumped out by the fire brigade and we paddled more conveniently in the streets than in the sea. On the second occasion I was awaiting embarkation in a wooden-hutted Army camp near Thetford. It was the winter of 1947, the coldest winter that even Norfolk had known for years, and the Army had cleverly arranged for the fuel to run out just before we arrived. We spent our time tearing down and smashing up anything that would burn. First the chairs, then the tables and the spare beds, and we were working our way through the roof joists by the time we moved out. I often wonder how the next occupants fared and which collapsed first, them or the roof.

After such inclement experiences it might be thought a trifle eccentric to return voluntarily to such a climate, and indeed even in a mild winter Norfolk can be pretty bleak, with only a few flat fields and the open sea between you and the Arctic Circle. There was rarely a February when roads were not blocked and pipes frozen, and in our worst winter the snow filled lanes to the tops of the hedges, villages were cut off for days, while in our pantry the eggs solidified and cracked their shells and the pickled onions froze in their vinegar.

It was not the weather which occupied me when I arrived at Norwich Thorpe station on that first Sunday and set off into the hinterland of mid-Norfolk on the leisurely local bus. Far more important, as we meandered through the empty landscape around Costessey and East Tuddenham and Mattishall, was that this was a far cry indeed from Hendon Magistrates' Court and Wembley Town Hall, and even further from that 8.10 to Trafalgar Square.

Dereham is one of Norfolk's most thriving market towns, the focal point of commercial, agricultural and social life for the whole of mid-Norfolk. It was a principal outpost of the Norfolk News Company, being the location of one of the district offices which served also the company's string of eight weekly papers, scattered all over the county from the *Beccles and Bungay Journal* on the Suffolk border up to the *North Norfolk News* based on Cromer and Sheringham. Mostly these offices were manned by just one or two district reporters, but the *Dereham & Fakenham Times* boasted its own editor, with two reporters to assist him in Dereham and another senior man in the Fakenham office, twelve miles away. Between the four of us we covered an area equivalent to most of Greater London, but in population terms about half the size of Luton.

The editor at that time was Maurice Woods, an untypical East Anglian with the lean and saturnine features and thin black moustache of a Spanish grandee, were it not for the Sherlock Holmes pipe and the ancient felt hat. Maurice could write either in elegant English or in phonetical Norfolk, and his weekly 'News from Dumpton', which read like a foreign language to me, constantly delighted his Norfolk followers. I did get the hang of it in the end, with its mawthers and dickeys and games of bowels; I even went around saying 'Hoold you haard togather bor', and 'Thass a rum owld do'. It impressed them back in the Edgware Road, but no Norfolkman was ever deceived.

Running the Fakenham office was one of the great characters of Norfolk journalism, Freddie Fletcher, who was there long before I arrived and as I write is working there still, no doubt continuing to curl that thread of hair between his fingers, though even while I was there the thread had retreated from over the forehead to behind the ear. He and Maurice were old friends, and since the other reporter at Dereham, Diana Standley, was a local girl I was very much the furriner and very much, I suspect, on trial.

Gently they guided me through the subtleties of rural reporting. Some of it of course had its Wembley equivalent – the magistrates' court, the local council, the occasional inquest. What made it so different, and gave it an atmosphere so much more pleasant than that of the impersonal world of suburbia, was that as the months went by I got to know personally the magistrates and the councillors and the coroner; more often than not I knew the defendants and the deceased as well. For a reporter this can be a mixed blessing. It is sometimes difficult to be entirely objective, and small local matters can sometimes get out of perspective. On the other hand it can give a better

21

understanding of a situation and lead to better informed, better balanced reporting if one knows something about the people and places involved.

Any position of responsibility can be misused, and it is possible for a country town reporter to be influenced by what his friends or the local hierarchy want him to print. But while not all of them are the sort of crusading local journalist who gets his office blown up in the third reel, I never met any in Norfolk who did not appreciate his responsibility to the profession as well as to the community in which he worked.

News-gathering was a joy in this kind of world, where a walk across the Market Place could take half an hour as you paused for a chat here and a word or two there. Over a pint in the King's Arms I could pick up enough ideas to fill a couple of columns, and in the cattle market on a Friday I could fill a couple more. It all took a little time, because there are a lot of pauses in Norfolk conversation, considerable periods of contemplation and silent thought, and often I have impetuously chipped in with another question as the minutes have ticked by, only to receive a continuation of the answer to the previous one. This is not because of any sluggishness of thought, it is merely the process of assessing first the questioner and then the question before phrasing an appropriate reply. It may give the impression of a certain dourness, a reluctance to respond, but I soon found that there is a shrewdness, a good-heartedness and a humour among Norfolkmen which the casual visitor might never suspect.

I reaped the full benefit of this when I moved out of my digs in Dereham – Miss Bunting had made me welcome, but digs are digs the world over – to set up home in the village of North Elmham, five miles away. Pat and I were married back in Harrow on 2 June 1951. With what care I filled in that wedding form for the *Wembley News*, and with what relief I found that the old days of juggling with the 'intro' were over and that the report started simply: 'The wedding took place at Christ Church, Roxeth, on Saturday . . .'

We bought a terraced cottage in the main street of North Elmham, three hundred years old and riddled with every kind of beetle, with a sagging pantile roof and a bulge or two in the walls. I doubt if a building society would have looked twice at it, but the Clerk to Mitford & Launditch Rural District Council came round for a drink, admired the oak beams and recommended the loan. It was a very civilised procedure, and what is more he knew his Norfolk cottages, because it stands there still and will last another century or so, I have no doubt.

It did have its drawbacks though. There was electricity, but no gas, no mains water, no sewerage. We pumped water from the well by the back door, on washing day we lit a fire beneath the big copper boiler in the outhouse, and once a week the night soil men came to empty the bucket at the far end of the garden. If we had too many visitors, then I had to empty it myself. For Pat, fresh from her hygienic years in London hospitals, it was quite a contrast, while my parents feared for my health, if not for my sanity. In fact they never did brave the horrors of that bucket, but insisted on staying at the local pub and visiting us for carefully limited periods. Inside the cottage there was an oak-beamed lounge with a big open hearth, where the log fire never really went out from October until March, and up the little winding stairs (so little and so winding that all the bedroom furniture had to go in through the window) we had two reasonable rooms and two tiny hutches under the eaves to accommodate all our incredulous London friends who could not believe we had actually gone native.

Happiness is a sagging roof and a pump outside the kitchen door. Early married life at Windfall Cottage, North Elmham.

We spent five years there, and we enjoyed ourselves no end. We called it Windfall Cottage – nothing to do with apples, just an oblique tribute to the compensation money that provided the down payment. In the process of learning how to run it, never an easy task for newly-weds, and with extra complications from the primitive plumbing, we discovered just how helpful and friendly a Norfolk villager can be. George and Molly Kerrison next door were shining examples. George ran the village shop and, more discreetly, most of the village as well. He it was who showed me how to replace a pantile, how to work the pump and nail the fence, and where to empty that grisly bucket. I think he reckoned we were a pretty feckless pair; when visitors failed to find us and asked him where we were, he used to tell them, 'I expect they're playing with the dog in the garden' – and quite often we were. He and Molly helped us with many an unfamiliar problem and introduced us to their friends in the village; although we never became 'locals', we were at least accepted and made welcome.

Village life fitted in well with my reporting duties. I became a commuter after all, not on the 8.10 to Trafalgar Square, but on a peaceful ten-minute drive along empty country lanes, somewhere between 9.30 and 10 o'clock. Home again for lunch on the quieter days (and no day was particularly noisy), and if the evening was free of meetings or club dinners then we might go to the whist drive in the Memorial Institute, or Pat might attend her WI meeting while I took a glass at the George and Dragon and watched the local bowls team. We had even acquired a dog to keep Pat company when she was not out visiting or helping in George's shop. The Pooch was one of a litter of puppies found deserted under a hedge, a sort of cross between a fox and a whippet. He looked a scruffy little thing, and he continued to look scruffy throughout the thirteen years we had him, but we loved him dearly.

The other members of the family at that time were a cat called Mitten, acquired from the village doctor just across the road, and Ancient Agatha the Staggering Standard, acquired from a shrewd fellow in Dereham who must have seen me coming. Agatha was undoubtedly the worst buy in the history of second-hand car sales. It was a sixteen-year-old Standard 8, and he asked £150 for it, which was no mean sum in 1951. I beat him down to £147, thinking myself no end of a clever fellow, and in the next three years spent double that just to hold it together. Finally the big end burst through the side of the engine and I sold Agatha to the scrap man for a tenner.

Still we had a lot of fun with Agatha. Any journey was an adventure, and the start of the annual excursion to London had all the tension and drama of a lift-off at Cape Canaveral. On one occasion it took us six hours to cover the hundred miles, limping along lopsidedly on a broken spring with every passing motorist shouting helpfully, 'Do you know your spring's broken?' The springs were all so fragile that going over a hump-backed bridge sounded like dropping a canteen of cutlery, as one of my bruised passengers once observed, and the wooden floorboards were so rotten that one girl reporter, entirely charming but generously built, managed to put her feet clean through them. Her legs thus protruded beneath the chassis as if providing some primitive form of additional propellant, which indeed in Agatha's case would not have come amiss.

Agatha not only conveyed me between Dereham and Elmham, she also played her part for the *Dereham & Fakenham Times*. We had a rather bizarre car fleet at that time – Di Standley, for instance, turned up at funerals in a dashing little red sports car – so nobody seemed to think it strange that my battered old wreck should bear a Press notice on the windscreen, and club secretaries all over mid-Norfolk grew accustomed to appealing for volunteers at the end of annual meetings to give that reporter fellow a shove with his car.

It was in Agatha that Pat and I first discovered some of those corners of Norfolk which the casual visitor rarely finds. Indeed the casual visitor himself is pretty rare, because Norfolk does little to encourage him. It offers few amenities outside the obvious resorts, it likes to cultivate the impression of having a flat and featureless terrain and, since it is not on the way to anywhere, few travellers pass through accidentally. Norfolkmen always used to say that they were cut off from the world by the North Sea and the London and North Eastern Railway. It was said not with bitterness but with relief.

So not too many people know about the rhododendron woods at Weasenham, for instance, or the lovely stretches of river through Elsing and Lyng, or the gorse-covered downs behind Burnham Deepdale. Even on the coast the sailing folk stay around Blakeney and Brancaster Staithe, children prefer Cromer, the trippers descend on Yarmouth and the Broads. I vow they have never stood on the beach at Titchwell at low tide, separated from the nearest road by a mile of salt marsh and an unmarked footpath, the sands a quarter-mile wide from sea wall to sea edge and stretching away to the horizon in either direction. You can turn full circle there and see not a soul, just the gulls and the oystercatchers and an occasional kingfisher over the marshes. At mid-morning on a sunny weekend in August, where else in Britain could offer that?

From all this it must be clear that I am slightly dotty about Norfolk. It is easier, though, to enthuse as a foreigner, even a foreigner who has lived there for years, than as a native Norfolkman, particularly one who works on the land. There is still a feudal atmosphere in some parts of the county, where the relationship between squire and villager has altered little in a hundred years. 'County' folk in Norfolk are very 'county' indeed: visiting one of the big halls to report on a hunt ball, I was asked to go round to the tradesmen's entrance. No doubt had I been a local man I would have gone there anyway.

Many of the farm cottages, at any rate back in the fifties, were unattractive, isolated and primitive, miles from a shop or a school. That bucket was a bit of a giggle at Windfall Cottage, but for many it was the normal way of life. Most farm workers could not afford even an Ancient Agatha in those days, but had to rely on the spasmodic public transport or more generally a bike. Even in the villages life was not too picturesque. The local pub sold beer and little else, because the licensee often worked on the land for his steady income and took the pub for a roof over his head. He had no time for fripperies like bar snacks and tablecloths and decorations behind the bar, and at lunchtime pubs were often cheerless places, with not even a fire in the hearth. Only in the evenings, when the day's work was over for landlord and customer alike, did the dominoes and the dartboard come out, and the pub itself come alive. Village schools were often in outdated, inadequate premises, with sports facilities limited to the school yard in spite of the acres of land all around. The village halls could offer little except whist and bingo; the bright lights of Dereham, with its one cinema and its Saturday dances, could be an hour's bike ride away.

Life on the land in Norfolk was no idyll in the nineteen-fifties, and small wonder that many youngsters were eager to leave it, but for a newly-wed young reporter with a job that he enjoyed and the fairly respectable income of £7 14s 2d a week, living in a cottage that was tied to no one but the treasurer's department of Mitford & Launditch RDC, with no children yet to educate and no transport problems as long as Agatha's wheels could be kept turning, Norfolk offered many attractions. I have never lost my affection for it.

Even rural reporting has its more wearisome duties. Each winter Saturday, for instance, I stood on the Dereham touchline, windswept or soaked or frozen, sometimes all three, charged with writing fifty words at half-time, followed in due course by the result. Those fifty words came hard at first, since there had only been Rugby at school and I had not seen a soccer match since I was twelve, but the standard phrases soon began to flow: 'Dereham kept up the pressure and Tufts beat the custodian with a first-time shot into the rigging', and so on. If in doubt there was always the invaluable 'End-to-end-play then ensued'. As long as I got the result right nobody really cared, because they knew I knew nothing about the game, and I knew they knew.

The real bane of a district reporter's life, and I hope it is less prevalent now than it was then, was taking mourners' names at funerals. Every name printed is another paper sold, so I fear the practice will die hard, but this was the task I liked least, not only because of the sheer embarrassment of intruding on such occasions, but also because these lists were fraught with hazards. Hell hath no fury like a mourner scorned; one name omitted, or misspelt, or in the wrong order of precedence, and even the deceased must have felt the reverberations. Even the wink from the undertaker, a regular drinking companion, as he led the cortege past me did not really relieve the tedium of it all.

If possible we left such duties to the village correspondents, most of whom enjoyed themselves vastly on these occasions because they knew most of the mourners' names without asking, and anyway any Norfolkman enjoys a good funeral. It could also be fairly lucrative at tuppence a line, and there was one such stalwart whose funerals were always heavily attended: a veritable army seemed to gather at the church to offer condolences. It was always, we noted, the same army, since the names rarely differed from funeral to funeral. For many months we assumed that this was a particularly devout and close-knit community, until we discovered that our correspondent made up the numbers by including the names of all the gravestones as well. 'That hen't wrarng,' he assured us when taxed about his unorthodox journalistic approach. 'They're all there togather in the chutchyard, they just hen't a-sayin' much.' We let it go.

Thus I learned the charms of working on a country paper. In my spare time I joined Round Table, a convivial gathering of under-forties and part of a movement founded in Norwich less than fifty years ago which is now world-wide. I found it a tremendous boon in later years to arrive in Lusaka or Bulawayo and to be able to contact local Tablers who made me immediately at home.

Even my early theatrical aspirations were able to blossom in mid-Norfolk, an area which might be thought not just the sticks but the stubble. The Dereham Players were exceptional by most amateur standards in having a professional producer, Frank Harwood, who rehearsed them not just once or twice a week, as has to suffice for most amateur companies, but every night for a gruelling three weeks, with a full week's run at the end of it. This achieved an unusually high standard of performance, though I say it (and frequently wrote it) myself, but it did present problems for a cast which had full-time jobs to fit in as well, particularly when that job, like mine, involved evenings. There was the further complication that Maurice Woods shared my affection for the greasepaint and was also a Dereham Player. The two of us, obviously, could never take so much time off simultaneously, so we never appeared together. Instead we worked out a sort of rota: Maurice mostly played a 'heavy' in the serious plays – I recall his chilling performance in *Gaslight*, when that sinister face, straight out of the Inquisition, sent many a coachload of Women's Institutes shivering to their beds–while I cavorted in the lighter productions, like the inevitable *See How They Run* and *Happiest Days of Your Life*. My farewell appearance was as Elwood P. Dowd in *Harvey*, which produced a plague of enormous white cardboard rabbits all over Dereham, to the considerable alarm of non-playgoers who thought that the current myxamatosis outbreak had taken a particularly unpleasant turn.

With the Players and Round Table as well as my reporting duties and all the other friends we had made, life developed into a congenial round of business mixed with pleasure or, more often, pleasure mixed with business. Maurice moved on in due course to the *Guardian*, to return later as London correspondent for the

Norfolk News Company's *Eastern Daily Press*, though his 'News from Dumpton' continued to be filed each week, whether from Manchester or London EC4. For a couple of years the pace quickened in the Dereham office under his successor, Don Brooks.

Don was a devoted journalist whose enthusiasm for the job, while not always appreciated by his staff, made a considerable impact on the town and the paper. He was the nearest I met to that crusading hero of the movies, fully prepared to risk a bomb in the letterbox or a knife between the shoulder blades for the sake of a good cause and a good story. He would have been happier in Dodge City than in Dereham, which was fairly short on wicked cattle barons and crooked sheriffs. As it was, no story was too trivial to escape his attention, and he would pursue the most obscure of leads with a terrifying tenacity. No bombs or knives resulted, just a few bags under our eyes and a certain amount of muttering under our breath, but he taught us all a lesson in thoroughness which did us no harm at all.

After Don's departure, and once we had gathered our breath, I was promoted to reporter-in-charge; the title of Editor, with its appropriate emolument, had somehow disappeared. This meant that we moved into the company house in Dereham, strategically placed behind Woolworths and only a minute's walk from the office. Windfall Cottage, now with mains water and soon to have main drainage, had obviously increased in value and we managed to sell it, with our usual business acumen, for three hundred pounds less than we had paid for it. It must have been the only property deal in Britain, at that time of acute housing scarcity, where the seller actually lost money. It changed hands recently for just twelve times what we sold it for, but now they call it Windfall House – that must have been where I went wrong.

Soon after the move our household was increased by one. Our first son was born in Dereham in September 1956, the only genuine Norfolkman in the family. We called him Jeremy John, mainly because we liked the names, though it also crossed my mind that 'J.J.' might look good one day at the top of a column or the foot of a chairman's memo. On the evening of his arrival I felt it my duty to spread the good tidings throughout every licensed establishment in the town. I remember very little of the last half a dozen pubs, but I am told I eventually made my regular evening call at the police station, enquired as usual 'Any news tonight?', then collapsed unconscious across the counter.

Other extra-mural activities also flourished. In Round Table I became secretary, then chairman, then area secretary. In the Players I was being given some plum parts. In the town I was getting a certain amount of gratifying attention, and in the county they were even letting me use the front door. In fact I was enjoying every aspect of being a medium-sized fish in a fairly small pool. And yet, and yet . . .

Perhaps it started when I found myself attending the football club's annual meeting for the eighth successive year (and for the eighth time seeing all the officers re-elected en bloc). Perhaps it was the hundredth local council meeting, or the umpteenth village fete. Certainly somewhere between a Tittleshall British Legion dinner and a Bawdeswell and District Bowls League final, I began to wonder whether all this was going to retain its lustre for another thirty years.

I began to realise that they would never need a Swaffer around Swaffham, although I find no fault with this. It was a life I had revelled in for eight years, and it was difficult at that stage to decide on anywhere I would rather be. I could see no advantage in moving to another provincial paper, and I was not at all sure by now that I wanted Fleet Street, nor that Fleet Street would want me, since my occasional glimpses of the way it operated filled me with neither admiration nor envy. Yet the nagging feeling persisted that before I settled irrevocably into my comfortable and not unrewarding routine I should make just one attempt to enter the larger world outside, if only to vindicate the glowing opinion of M. Young, Captain RA.

There seemed to be only one branch of journalism where the unpredictable excitements of front-rank reporting could be combined with security and a reasonable civility. Without any great optimism I started scanning *World's Press News* again, this time for vacancies in the BBC.

Chapter Four

My ambitions ran no higher at that stage than the newly-opened
BBC studios in Norwich, but it so happened that in the autumn of
1958, under the heading 'Public Appointments' – only in the BBC
could a reporter's job be called a 'public appointment' – there
appeared this invitation:

> BBC require reporter, News Division. Candidates must have
> journalistic experience, good news sense, wide knowledge of
> current affairs and ability to write accurate, concise reports for
> bulletins and to broadcast their own reports in Sound and
> Television. Possibility of short-term assignments abroad . . .
> Starting salary £1,105.

It seemed ludicrously presumptuous even to look at it twice.
'Journalistic experience' was all right, if you counted a dozen
years of darts club dinners. 'Good news sense' I might just get
away with; I knew that man-bites-dog rated higher than dog-
bites-man, though in Dereham we were still waiting for it to
happen. But what about 'wide knowledge of current affairs'? I
rarely got further than Beachcomber in the *Daily Express*, and
'current affairs' in Norfolk meant mostly the latest prices for fat
cattle, or how the rain was affecting the barley. As for
'broadcasting reports in Sound and Television' – the BBC always
put capital letters on those awesome words – would a school
elocution prize and six performances as Elwood P. Dowd qualify
me as the new Ed Murrow? I filled in the four pages of the
application form with an increasing sense of desperation. 'In
connection with speaking and appearing in public,' I wrote, 'I
have played major roles in numerous amateur productions, the
most recent of these being the lead in *Harvey*. That's one up on Mr
Murrow, I thought. I bet he never interviewed a six-foot invisible
rabbit.

A month after the application went off, with still no word in
reply, I resigned myself not too regretfully to becoming the

31

Norfolk News Company's longest-serving district reporter. After all, I assured myself, everyone knows that the only way into the BBC is through Eton and Oxbridge or playing tennis with the Director-General's daughter. These advertisements were merely published to create a facade of fairness and to satisfy the unions.

It was in mid-November, well into the British Legion dinner season, and I was again beginning to look like a steak and kidney pie, when the appointments department of the BBC came to life. Sir Herbert Thompson advised me that he would be grateful for my presence at a written and recorded test, the written section to be of one and a quarter hours' duration. Sir Herbert would be pleased to refund my return railway fare (second class) and any other reasonable expenses I might incur in accordance with the enclosed scale. This was my first encounter with Corporation correspondence and I was deeply impressed. To have my application dealt with by a knight was in itself rather gratifying, let alone have him pay my train fare, but how splendid to have such split-second timing – one and a quarter hours, not a minute more or less, and that precise scale of expenses, costed to the last penny. Here was confirmation that the BBC must be a smooth-running, well organised, highly efficient machine. I was still, of course, extremely young.

There was no hint in the letter of what the test involved. I visualised a kind of 'Brain of Britain' affair, a complex general knowledge quiz conducted perhaps in several languages ('possibility of short-term assignments abroad'). In the week before the test I pored over every paper that Dereham Library could offer me, from the share prices in the *Financial Times* to the illicit liaisons in the *News of the World*. A wide knowledge of current affairs they wanted, and wide it was going to be.

As it turned out, the test was entirely straightforward and for me entirely unexpected. We were given a typewriter and some paper, and told simply to write a report on any news story we had recently covered. Double spacing, one side of the paper only, and of course exactly one and a quarter hours. Around me, stories began to be unfolded of terrible earthquakes in Turkey, of plane crashes and mine disasters and great political dramas, brilliant encapsulations of sensational world events. With a sinking heart I reviewed the great stories of the day that had recently engaged my professional attention, and wrote a thousand words on the use of waste land for growing Christmas trees.

It had looked quite a lively story in the *Dereham & Fakenham Times*. An enterprising horticulturist just outside Dereham, Peter Fitt of Gorgate Hall, had shown me how he had filled up some 'scutes' of barren land with little spruce trees and was making them a profitable concern. Even the *Eastern Daily Press* had run half a column. Here in the bowels of Portland Place, nerve centre of one of the greatest news-gathering organisations in the world, the story seemed somehow to lose its drama.

They led us individually into a studio to record our masterpieces, and as I heard myself explaining into the microphone the more obscure characteristics of the sitka spruce I knew that this broadcasting business was not for me. I took myself off to the nearest pub to incur some reasonable expenses, and returned to Norfolk grateful for Sir Herbert's hospitality and quite looking forward to my next Legion dinner.

Somewhere in the BBC Appointments Department there must have been a horticulturist who had not appreciated before how to make use of his 'scutes', or maybe a Christmas tree dealer in need of a new source of supply. It may have been the good Sir Herbert himself, whom I later discovered to have relatives in Norfolk and whose recreations in *Who's Who* include gardening. However it happened, two weeks later I was called back for an interview with the Appointments Board itself.

I recall only one question from that interview. Someone representing the Civil Service Commissioners asked me what Sunday paper I read, and nodded approvingly when I told him, not being a complete idiot, the *Sunday Times*. He made no other contribution to the discussion, having presumably established to the satisfaction of the Civil Service that I was neither a Communist nor a sex maniac.

Three days later came phase three, a screen test at Alexandra Palace, with the train fares and reasonable expenses now mounting up into quite a sizeable investment for the Corporation. Having learned all about screen tests from Hollywood musicals, I went prepared to perform the closing scene from *Harvey* or, if they preferred, the farewell speech of the doomed Duke of Clarence, heavy fall and all.

Alexandra Palace, that gaunt mausoleum perched above the Victorian roof-tops of Hornsey and Muswell Hill, bears little resemblance to Paramount Studios, and the screen test fell rather short of those in which Deanna Durbin always did so well. I had to interview the BBC's deputy industrial correspondent, Alan Wheatley, on the relationship between managements and trade unions, a subject as familiar to me then as whale-hunting in the Antarctic. Happily Alan is a kindly man, well aware of how intimidating a television studio can be, and he did not try to catch me with monosyllabic answers or baffling expertise, nor did he toss back that googly of a counter-question, 'What exactly do you mean by that?' When I displayed the vacant stare of an interviewer who cannot think of the next question, he gallantly kept talking until I did. It was a very gentle ride indeed, and now that he is head of public relations for the Electricity Council I hope that the Press treat him just as tolerantly when he has to explain the next price rise. The other part of the test was to read my Christmas tree saga into the camera, and I felt I gave it all the sincerity and depth of feeling of a ministerial broadcast. Fortunately it was by now only a week before Christmas, and the whole thing became suddenly topical. When I had finished, the floor manager asked me where he could get hold of a dozen at wholesale prices. The feeling grew that, miraculously, I was home and dry.

It was not until mid-January 1959, after a period in which every glimpse of a Christmas tree added to the suspense, that the final letter came. Carefully I picked my way through the crucial paragraph:

> . . . Grade B1 on the unestablished staff, starting salary rising subject to satisfactory service by basic annual increments of £55 to an efficiency line of £1,270, above which if you are regarded by the Corporation as being of a satisfactory standard of efficiency you can expect to progress beyond it to a roof of £1,550 receiving the higher rate of increments where it applies . . .

I gathered I had got the job.

The contract that followed was even more formidable. 'You agree to devote the whole of your time and attention to the service of the Corporation,' it said coldly, 'and to attend for duty at such hours of the day or night and at such place or places in the United Kingdom of Great Britain and Northern Ireland as shall from time to time be decided by the Corporation.' (The significance of that reference to Northern Ireland escaped me at the time.) 'You also agree,' it went on remorselessly, 'to undertake such periods of travel and service abroad as may be required by the Corporation . . . and you agree at all times to exercise your talent to the best of your skill and ability in the interests of the Corporation, to observe all instructions given to you and to conform to all rules and regulations of the Corporation for the time being in force . . .'

What a jolt this was after the easy-going life of a Norfolk district reporter. This was Auntie BBC with the mittens off. Was I joining a news organisation or the Foreign Legion? What's more, the Norfolk News Company had just offered me (by coincidence, they said, and I believe them completely) a pay rise which would bring me to within a hundred pounds of the BBC's offer, with none of the expense or inconvenience of moving to a much more costly existence in less attractive surroundings among complete strangers. It was a moment to pause awhile for careful and deliberate thought.

By return post I advised Sir Herbert that I was on my way.

The BBC News Division was based in Egton House, a rather seedy pile alongside Broadcasting House, long since demolished now and replaced by a glass and concrete rectangle which still bears the name. I shared a homely little office with Christopher Jones, a former Press Association man who had completed the entry course simultaneously with me and whose immaculate shorthand, combined with some rather dashing waistcoats, soon took him into Parliamentary reporting. He was later to become a regular member of the BBC's Westminster team and in due course chairman of the Parliamentary Press Gallery. At that time, though, we were both just new boys, privileged to join a rather select little coterie of BBC staff correspondents and reporters whose names and faces were already familiar on Sound and Television. Doyen of the group was Godfrey Talbot, former war reporter, now Court correspondent, later to become my mentor and guide in the world of the gentle handclasp and the slightly bowed head. Bert Mycock was the current industrial expert, with Alan Wheatley, my friendly neighbourhood interviewee, as his deputy. Reginald Turnhill was there, recently transformed from industrial to air correspondent, an unlikely conversion on the face of it, since a knowledge of industrial relations does not necessarily lead to a familiarity with aeroplanes; but then a previous industrial correspondent had become our man in

Beirut, so who can forecast where a grounding in union procedure may lead? Roland Fox and Conrad Voss-Bark were our political and parliamentary correspondents, rarely emerging from their Westminster fastness, and there the specialisation ended. The rest of us were all-purpose reporters, not yet segregated into science or education or home affairs. These titles were to come much later, the result partly of the challenge of independent television, where every reporter seemed to bear some sort of label, and partly of some industrious empire-building by individual reporters themselves. For some of them, as is so often the case in the BBC, it happened entirely by accident. John Burns, for instance, went to the Rome Olympics as a spare reporter, covered the cycling events because none of the sporting experts could be bothered, and has been the BBC's cycling correspondent ever since.

Among the 'leg-men' of those days were four future foreign correspondents. The tall and sardonic Gerald Priestland was to go to Washington, the dumpy and genial Angus McDermid was to follow him after a spell in Africa, and the eloquent Donald Milner and immaculate Ronald Robson were to succeed each other in various posts from Nairobi to Delhi. David Holmes was to become political editor, Leonard Parkin went into newscasting with ITN, Ray Colley went into top administration in the north, and John Tidmarsh was to anchor 'Today's' companion evening programme, 'Newsdesk'. My arrival created complications for John, since our names were constantly confused by the public. The appearance some years later of John Simpson has not helped to make things any clearer. To my delight there were also two East Anglians in the team, Peter Hardiman Scott and Douglas Brown, both of whom will still lapse into dialect at the drop of a dumpling. Peter Scott, who dropped the 'Peter' for broadcasting purposes to avoid confusion with his bird-watching namesake – should I have helped John Tidmarsh by broadcasting as Harry Timpson? – worked his way up through the Westminster office to become the Director-General's chief assistant, and Douglas carved himself an ecclesiastical niche to become religious affairs correspondent, the Friar Tuck of Radio News, to the considerable awe, I suspect, of his old colleagues on the *Eastern Daily Press*.

Together they comprised a rather gentlemanly group, presided over by a Reporting Organiser called Tom Maltby, a genial father figure who acted as guide, protector and general wet nurse to the lads under his command. Tom was a master of Corporation diplomacy. If any directives came down concerning his 'boys' of which he did not approve – extra duties, perhaps, or criticism of our expense sheets – he would accept the instruction, express his entire agreement, enforce it for a suitable period, then gently let it lapse. On the other hand, if he wished to press for some measure on our behalf, such as more office space or better equipment, he knew precisely who should be sent a formal memo, who should receive copies of it, and who should just be discreetly plied with ale in the BBC Club bar, If some administrative idiocy inflamed us into rebellion, he would head off our frontal assaults and conduct his own devious campaign round the flank. He fought many battles for us in the mysterious corridors of Corporation power and rarely returned the loser. Most of all, he had a great belief in the status and prestige of the radio reporter, and he impressed this not only on other people in News Division but on us reporters as well. He imbued a certain esprit into our little corps as we chuckled over him, and tried to live up to him.

Tom gave me my first BBC pep-talk: 'Never hesitate to come to me for help, lad. I'm always here, sitting on the network.' He sent me my first BBC memo, advising me that I should devote myself first to 'familiarisation with the technicalities, geography and personalities of News Division'. He was also the first person for many years, outside my immediate family, to address me as John. Ever since prep-school, right through the *Wembley News* and National Service and all the time in Norfolk, it had been 'Timmy'. Pat and her family always called me that, even my own sister took to using it, and indeed they still do. It was this resumed use of my long-ignored Christian name, perhaps more than the new job itself, which made me feel that a new era had begun.

On the technical side, the News Division was changing from discs to tape. I just missed the period in which steel wire was used for recordings, on spools so enormous that two of them threaded on an iron bar might have taxed a professional weightlifter. Tape recordings were still regarded with suspicion – they were too easily wiped, the tape could stretch, the machines needed too much time to run up speed – so for recording studio reports we still cut discs, always in duplicate so that sections could be deleted by switching from one machine to another. One 'fluff' meant two fresh discs, and another guinea on the bill for the licence-payer. It was an expensive and laborious process. Party conferences, for instance, which were recorded complete, produced three or four hundred discs. Those that were not kept for the archives could only be thrown away. At least it did teach us when recording our reports to get it right the first time, and it was gratifying, I suppose, to know that we reporters probably cut more discs in a year than all the pop stars put together.

For outside reporting, however, they were just introducing tape, and we were issued with what they euphemistically called a 'Midget' portable tape-recorder, which was not very portable and certainly no midget but a great step forward from the old converted limousines with disc-recording equipment which had previously been the only way of interviewing anyone outside the studios. The 'Midget' weighed ten pounds officially, but at the end of a long day felt more like ten hundredweight. It was a rectangular green box, on the same lines as an Army ammunition box and only slightly smaller. The microphone used with it was a great bulbous affair, too large for even a poacher's pocket, and thus a dead giveaway on occasions when one would have preferred a certain anonymity. All the same the 'Midget' was a major step in making reporters mobile and independent of the more cumbersome machinery provided by Outside Broadcasts. It could also be used to advantage, I discovered, in creating a passage through crowds: one shrewd blow behind the knees with it and the bulkiest obstruction could be felled like a log.

In the studio I learned how to avoid rustling papers under a microphone, how to enter and leave a studio silently, how to pour a glass of water without it going glup, how to read at the official BBC speed of three words to the second – all the basic rules of broadcasting which even in those days, as I recall, the 'Today' programme totally ignored.

'Familiarisation with the geography' was not too difficult, since we occupied only a modest corner of Egton house, and to this day I have no idea who occupied the floors above and below. We entered Broadcasting House itself only to visit the canteen. The two buildings were connected by a subway under the road, and the far end of that subway was to me a remote and mysterious grotto, peopled by strange tribes called Drama, and Light Entertainment, and Features. We in News Division never spoke of them; they were the showbiz side of broadcasting, while we were involved in the real world outside. Even the newsreaders, distinguished figures though they were, did not rate as real newsmen. During my 'familiarisation with personalities' a reporter described them to me as 'the stud bulls of broadcasting – put anything in front of them and they'll work their way through it'. I suspect that John Snagge and Frank Phillips and Alvar Lidell would hardly have appreciated that thought, yet in its way it was a tribute to their professionalism. They could make poetry of the most mundane prose, and on the big occasions no voice in the world could surpass them.

Although today the reporter voice piece is an integral part of the main news bulletins, in those days we left it to the newsreaders and our main outlet was that splendid wartime veteran, 'Radio Newsreel'. Still among the most prestigious of new programmes on the BBC's External Services, it has, alas, long since been eliminated from the domestic schedules. It went out at seven o'clock each evening, while nine or ten overseas editions went out right round the clock, and a permanent team of producers kept the machine functioning for twenty-four hours a day, seven days a week. It was half an hour of interviews, straight reports, and 'actuality', and it provided the foundation for every current affairs programme that radio has since produced. Its signature tune, 'Imperial Echoes', still gives me a special kind of jolt when I hear it abroad, and it must be familiar to every expatriate Englishman. Tom Maltby, a former producer on it himself, even named his house 'Echoes' in its honour.

To get three minutes in the lead spot on 'Radio Newsreel' was as satisfying as half a dozen voice pieces in bulletins today. Indeed, to get anything on it at all was quite an achievement, because there were other programmes to be filled by juniors like Chris Jones and me. There was a rather charming programme, for instance, called 'The Eyewitness', for which a reporter would be sent off to view an exhibition or to try out a new coach service or perhaps merely to amble round a bulb field or a mushroom farm, and then write a leisurely piece about his impressions. It was a programme into which my Christmas tree saga would have fitted like a glove, and I took to it with enthusiasm, particularly as it generally involved a day out in the country with all expenses paid.

My first actual broadcast was for another news programme, little publicised and rarely praised, but a splendid training ground for many who made a more spectacular mark in later years. This was the South-East Region News, the first radio home of people like Douglas Cameron, who was to humanise the humdrum world of roadworks and burst water mains for four years on 'Today'; of Bob Friend, another 'Today' character who later became BBC correspondent in Australia; and, most notable of all, of Marshall Stewart, who was to revolutionise the 'Today' programme at the start of the nineteen-seventies as editor of morning current affairs programmes. The editor of the regional news was Maurice Ennals, another of Auntie's father-figures, who became manager of the BBC's first local radio station in Leicester and later took over Radio Solent.

It was Maurice who gave me my first radio assignment: I was to voice a descriptive piece, duration one minute forty-five seconds, about a ship-spotters club in Margate. 'Ship-spotters' is a phrase with obvious hazards for the novice broadcaster, and I spent much time practising, lest a misplaced consonant should end my broadcasting career before it had begun. Apart from that there was little I needed to do in preparation, for in those well padded days the preparations were all made for us by a group of devoted BBC ladies who rejoiced in the corporate title of Facilities. They undertook all the preliminary planning, made the phone calls, booked the appointments, bought the tickets, and generally cosseted the reporters in a way I found entirely delightful. Thus, even for this modest expedition, a full brief was supplied. I have it still. 'Please go in the first place,' it said gently, 'to the Margate Information Bureau and liaise with Peter Bedford, the PRO. The Bureau is in Marine Terrace, only 200 yards from the railway station – turn left outside the station. He is expecting you at 12.15. Train leaves Victoria at 09.35, arriving Margate 11.45. Suggest you catch the 2.06 for return, getting in Victoria at 4.12. Railway voucher and other literature attached.'

In case I still failed to negotiate the intricacies of Southern Region, or turned right outside the station instead of left, a producer was detailed to accompany me. Alec Turnbull will probably not remember that trip, but I can still recall the excitement of my first journey in a first-class compartment, my first free lunch from a PRO, my first recorded interview 'for real', and then listening that evening to my first broadcast. It was also my first experience, incidentally, of how a shrewd PRO operates. Next morning a greetings telegram arrived at the office from

Peter Bedford. 'Congratulations,' it said, 'on a very fine first-timer last evening.' It was top-quality flannel, but I have had a soft spot for Peter ever since.

Chapter Five

After the gentle BBC indoctrination, the pace began gradually to quicken. I was let loose with my 'Midget', unchaperoned by any producer, to attend stone-laying ceremonies and statue unveilings and similar staple fare of the South-East Region News. The occasional minor politician was allotted to me for questioning, so I had my first encounters with that classic observation which has been handed out to newsmen since the Congress of Vienna: 'We had full and frank discussions on matters of mutual interest.' One or two items crept into 'Radio Newsreel', one of my pieces for 'The Eyewitness' was reproduced in the *Listener*, and an old lady in Brighton wrote to say how charming I sounded when I reported a London bank robbery. It was actually John Tidmarsh she meant, but I began to feel I had arrived.

The next familiarisation process was three months in the House of Commons as assistant to the political and parliamentary correspondents. It was a regular stint for general reporters in those days, and quite invaluable in providing an insight into Parliamentary procedure. On one memorable day, the legendary Churchill appeared there himself, to take that special seat of his below the gangway. A frail, unsteady figure, when he spoke his voice was little more than an inaudible growl, but I had grown up during the war when this man was to us schoolboys a Colossus towering over the nation, fending off our enemies with little more than two raised fingers. To see him there in the Commons, albeit only a sad and shrunken shadow of that hero we had followed, was an occasion to cherish over the years. In 1965 I was to join the sad vigil outside his home near Hyde Park, as the outside broadcast cameras waited through two days and nights for the final bulletin to come. When at last his death was announced and I had to stand outside the house under the arc lights to pass on the news, I had the feeling that every BBC reporter must experience from time to time, the feeling of participating in a moment of history.

During those three months in the House I learned a little about the funny ways of those who are elected to authority over us. When the first experimental broadcasts were made from Parliament the whole nation was able to hear that curious tribal chant that MP's so relish, the 'yar-yar-yar' and the interruptions and cries of 'Shame!' and 'Resign!' which give the effect, as I think John Snagge described it, of the final stages of a rowing club dinner. But the House also has an atmosphere uniquely suited to the great occasion, to a dramatic ministerial announcement or to a devastating exchange across the Despatch Box. I spent those first three months in the House alternately marvelling at the brilliance of the oratory and wincing at the banality of the heckling. I was deeply impressed by the adroitness of ministers at Question Time, but astonished at the emptiness of the benches during debates once the opening speeches were over. Just a handful of back-benchers would be left, hoping to make their mark in *Hansard* and thus, in due course, in their local Press. I learned the basic truths which apply as much to Parliament as to local councils: that it is not the man constantly on his feet in the Chamber who necessarily serves his constituents best, that the real hard graft is done privately in committee or simply behind an office desk, and that the soundest, hardest-working members are not always those with the most questions on the Order Paper, or the most mentions in *Hansard*, or indeed the most appearances on 'Today'.

It is a strange, isolated little world, up in the corridors behind the Press Gallery, a world of political gossip where an ill-chosen ministerial phrase can be expanded into a scare headline, and an indiscreet conversation can be used to rock a Government. I never quite fathomed the love-hate relationship which must exist between political writers and the politicians they write about, often so scathingly. They mock them and castigate them, and the politicians in their turn attack the media with bitterness and detestation, yet they all live together in the Palace of Westminster on genial, first-name terms, without a hint of personal rancour.

I had one more initiation to undergo before my 'familiarisation' was complete. After those three months in the rarified atmosphere of the Press Gallery I moved some eight miles northwards to a very different world, for three months at Alexandra Palace with Television News. Reporters worked equally for Sound and Television, in those days when both words still rated capitals. Indeed, television news seemed the poorer relation of the two, tucked away in its eyrie in North London, and much slower than radio news because of the sheer mechanics of filming and processing and editing. The prestige seems to have been transferred since the early Alexandra Palace days, though, and so skilled have television techniques become that even a two-day-old piece of film can be presented with tremendous urgency and aplomb.

Naturally I was thrilled to get among the cameras. This was rather closer to the old Palladium dream than inspecting an exhibition of posters for 'The Eyewitness'. There was no formal training here. The training was done by the cameramen out on the job as they stood you against the right background, told you where to look, warned you not to blink or shuffle about, and generally moulded you into a rather competent microphone stand.

The training ground for new reporters at Alexandra Palace was the visual equivalent of the South-East Region News, 'Town and Around', a rather cheery little fifteen minutes of local council controversies, art exhibitions and eccentric centenarians, on quiet evenings only half a step ahead of the *Dereham & Fakenham Times*. Not only did we film reports for it, we occasionally presented our own material in the studio, which was an excellent chance to acquire some experience in the adrenalin-and-ulcer world of live television.

My first television assignment was at Petworth House, where John Wyndham, later Baron Egremont, was opening some State rooms – or perhaps closing them, I was never really quite sure which. Like many other 'Town and Around' items, it was selected for the pictures rather than the story, and the reporter went along mainly to hold the lights. I was allowed, however, a brief appearance on the screen. By great good fortune a small girl joined the proceedings and provided some rather delightful light relief, which lifted the story slightly out of the routine of 'What a wonderful place you have here'. It earned the approval of my masters back at the Palace and, in the way these things happen, I as reporter took the credit for her performance.

In the studio I was able to watch the familiar figures at work – Robert Dougall, Kenneth Kendall, Richard Baker and Michael Aspel, the regular newsreading team. At the time I found it a little surprising, but vastly consoling, that all these veterans still showed signs of nervousness before they were actually on the air, and some years later I had the temerity to mention this to Bob Dougall. Surely, I said, after all these years there are not still butterflies in the tummy. Uncle Bob smiled that avuncular smile which has charmed so many millions. 'My boy,' he said, 'the day you stop having butterflies before you go on the air is the day you should give up broadcasting.'

Of course he was right. If broadcasting becomes so routine that you no longer worry about it, then it shows. The concentration goes, the interest fades, and the viewer or the listener loses interest too. Happily, even at 6.45 in the morning, my heart still gives a little flutter when that green light goes on.

The 'Town and Around' team got under way when the national news was over at six o'clock. One of the regular newsreaders generally presented it, but sometimes a story cropped up which the reporter himself introduced live in the studio. This led to my first encounter with that television cheat-box, the teleprompter. Other programmes use more sophisticated devices, but television news teleprompters are designed for rapid alterations or additions in the stories, and consist basically of a long narrow roll of paper on which the script is typed by the prompter girl. It fits into a box with a magnifying lens on the front, and the operator can then roll it behind the lens at whatever speed the newsreader is reading.

The effect is quite unnerving. Only two or three lines are visible at a time, only two or three words on each line, so it is easy to lose the gist of a complicated sentence, and to lose the breath too if it turns out to be longer than you expected. There is also the illusion that the roll is turning just that little bit faster than you are reading, so you accelerate a bit to catch up. The girl realises you are speeding up and turns the roll a little faster, so you speed up a bit more, and so on. The story goes that one novice newsreader, trapped in this visual rat-race, actually completed a fifteen-minute bulletin in nine minutes and thirty seconds.

Once the speed problem has been solved, there is the temptation to become too reliant on the prompter, which can have equally disastrous results. There are often gaps in a teleprompter script; a story may have arrived too late for the girl to include it, although new ones can be added even during the bulletin itself, or a piece of script which has to be read while film is being shown is not put on the prompter because the newsreader is out of vision anyway. What happens then is that you are reading confidently from the prompter when suddenly the neat little row of words end abruptly with a pencilled note: See Script. It is quite likely, however, that you have been failing to turn the pages of your script during that lengthy read from the prompter, and there is the heart-sinking experience of searching through the sheets while a film runs silently on or, worse still, while the eyes of millions watch your discomfiture. Having found the right page and the right place, you feel disinclined ever to chance losing it again, which means eyes down for a full bulletin.

Fortunately I never experienced the more dramatic hazards with teleprompters that the old hands can recall. One night, so it is said, the screw which adjusts the height of the prompter came loose, and as it sank lower and lower beneath the camera, so the newsreader sank lower and lower behind his desk. He read the final words with his head hunched well below his shoulders. On another occasion the prompter was accidentally knocked over, and as it keeled over sideways so the newsreader leaned over with it until he disappeared completely out of sight. Even when everything is working properly, it takes a lot of practice to read coherently from a teleprompter, and full marks to the experts who do it so well. Even years later, when I was reading the news regularly on bbc2, I still found it the trickiest piece of equipment to master.

There were other techniques to learn in those first three months at Alexandra Palace. Timing is so vital when film or videotape is involved, to ensure that the script exactly fits the pictures, that I had to get used to what I always thought of as writing in waltz-time. With the standard bbc reading speed set at three words to a second, we wrote our scripts three words to a line to make it easier to time them. This made for rather unnatural composition, especially when a film was so short that sentences had to be mercilessly clipped or so long that they had to be inordinately extended. Words were often chosen not for literary merit but merely to fit the pictures. It could be argued (and frequently is, by radio men) that while a radio bulletin is written on news values, a television bulletin is written on picture values. Television men would reply that for them the words are just one of the dimensions they work in, and that a two-dimensional bulletin must be that much more effective. It is an old argument in the bbc, and having worked in both camps I can support both sides. There is no doubt that words plus pictures can be more effective, but without the pictures you can certainly improve the words.

At the end of my three months at the Palace I was reluctant to leave. It had a unique atmosphere in those days, an outpost of the BBC empire which took advantage of its isolation to disregard many of the administrative formalities which more accessible departments in the Corporation had to observe. Our newsroom up in the tower had a finer view than any other BBC office in London. In the summer we could disport ourselves in the acres of grounds, and in the winter we had our own club bar and entertainments. Parking space was unlimited. Above all, these were still the formative years of television news, and the pioneering spirit of John Logie Baird had not entirely vanished. It was to be revived again a few years later when I returned to Alexandra Palace for the launch of the new-style bulletins on BBC2.

Meanwhile I returned to Egton house, now a fully fledged member of the reporting team and poised for assignments in Sound and Television anywhere in the world. I had been pumped full of assorted vaccines, I had my own 'Midget' and my Corporation stopwatch, my overnight bag was packed in the boot of my Corporation car, and I was ready to take my share of whatever jobs came along. I dined with the Victoria Cross Association, surrounded by heroes; reported the first night of the Proms, surrounded by streamers; and attended the opening of the new *Daily Mirror* building in Holborn, surrounded by liquor. I watched the unveiling of the Trenchard Memorial on the Embankment, I took my turn at the passing-out parades at Sandhurst and the flower shows at Chelsea, and when Mr Macmillan was given the freedom of the City at the Mansion House I was at the end of the table, working my way cheerfully – more and more cheerfully – through the Château Leoville Barton 1945 and the Krug 1952 and the Hine Grand Champagne 1935. If only the darts team from North Elmham could have joined me, alongside His Excellency the High Commissioner for the Federation of Rhodesia and Nyasaland and the Right Worshipful the Mayor of the City of Westminster, what a time we would have had.

Not all the assignments were so comfortable, of course, or went so smoothly. On one story I even redesigned Marble Arch. It was the fault of a certain Dr Barbara Moore, a remarkable woman very prone to walking considerable distances for reasons which I never entirely fathomed. It was my lot to accompany her on the final stage of one of these marathons, along the Edgware Road to the finishing point àt Marble Arch itself. Unfortunately, encumbered by my 'Midget', surrounded by a boisterous crowd, and sorely out of condition, I lost contact with the intrepid doctor and was left talking into my microphone some distance to the rear. Not daring to admit defeat, I continued my eyewitness commentary behind the backs of the crowd, including a detailed description of the now invisible Dr Moore, until a distant cheer advised me that she must have completed the course.

'And there she goes now,' I cried exultantly into my 'Midget' as I limped along the gutter, with not even the top of her head in sight. 'There she is, in her moment of triumph, mounting those great steps at Marble Arch.'

I hastened back to the studio, just in time to get the tape into the main news bulletin. Within minutes, half the population of Britain was telephoning to point out that at Marble Arch there were no great steps for Dr Moore to mount, indeed there were no steps there at all. I tried to suggest that they were symbolic steps I referred to, but nobody seemed convinced.

As the months went by I found I was not always at the back. I never really enjoyed foot-in-the door reporting, nor shoulder-in-the-gap or even microphone-through-the-legs. Apart from requiring a certain physical strength and considerable thickness of skin, it also seemed faintly un-British. I endured my quota of 'doorstepping', the tedious practice of accosting public figures on doorsteps to ask questions which you know they will not answer, and I also survived the scrimmages at news conferences and the scrambles at the airport. In due course I realised that my Press colleagues' feet and shoulders were not always heftier than mine, and that I had the advantage of a microphone to impress the interviewee and ten pounds of tape-recorder to thump into the competition. Those Olympian figures from Fleet Street whose by-lines filled the front pages turned out to be only human after all. Was it because I was getting as fly as they were?

The most significant of my assignments in that first year, which led to my only spell as a specialist correspondent in the BBC, were those involving the little green cards from Buckingham Palace or Clarence House, advising the populace that I was authorised to be granted facilities as a BBC 'observer' (the Court did not use words like 'reporter') at some specific royal occasion. I still have a hundred or so of these cards, permitting me to 'observe' events ranging from Princess Margaret opening a new garage in Woolwich (which she did with tremendous aplomb) to the Queen opening Parliament.

The early ones mostly involved just a brief descriptive piece for the South-East Region, the basic ingredients being a description of the royal dress (supplied by the lady-in-waiting), a few words from the royal speech (supplied by the press secretary), and if possible a little light relief (supplied mostly by me). By these devices I kept the loyal subjects in the south-east fully up-to-date with the movements of the Royal Family around their hospitals and churches and garages. There were also the airport arrivals and departures, meriting a few words in the bulletin: I welcomed the Queen Mother back from Rhodesia, saw the Queen off to India, and watched Prince Philip catching helicopters the way most of us catch taxis.

It was straightforward, undemanding work, occasionally repetitious but generally fairly comfortable, with sometimes a decent dinner thrown in. I got to know the two court correspondents from the Press Association and Exchange Telegraph, Ronnie Gomer-Jones and Louis Nickolls (known disrespectfully among their colleagues as Tweedledum and Tweedledee), and was sometimes privileged to share their limousine in the royal processions, helping them to turf out any local reporter who attempted to get on board. I learned how to bluff my way through police barriers in order to park my car, and the right moment to slip away from a tree-planting ceremony to make sure of my seat for lunch. The royal detectives, laden with their umbrellas and discarded royal overcoats, actually began to recognise me as I popped up from behind foundation stones and outside old people's homes. Even so, I had little suspicion then that I was earmarked for a six-year spell of royal engagements as the BBC's deputy accredited correspondent to the Court of St James, more pithily described by my colleagues as 'Number Two on the Royals'.

Chapter Six

I have always suspected that the BBC went about appointing a deputy Court correspondent in the same careful, methodical way it used to reserve for filling many such distinguished appointments – somebody looked in the reporters' room, I happened to be the only one there, and they said 'You'll do'. Of course it was all made to look more formal than that: in August 1960 the Assistant Editor, Teddy Thompson, sent me one of those splendid BBC memos (copies to ENCA, DENCA, RO, HOB/S), advising me of my selection as understudy to the Court correspondent and adding coldly: 'There is no question of our creating any specialised post – the idea is simply that we should regard one member of the staff as first choice for helping the Court correspondent when he needs it or standing in for him when he is not available.' Which was the BBC way of saying 'No extra pay'.

The Court correspondent, and Number One on the Royals, was of course Godfrey Talbot, senior member of the reporting team and by that time confidant of royalty and idol of the women's luncheon clubs. Godfrey held the office from soon after the war until he retired in 1973, and during that time covered nearly all the major activities of the royal family: it used to be said in the office that the BBC had made him responsible for every royal birth in a quarter of a century. Around 1960 royal births started becoming so plentiful, and other royal activities multiplied so much as well, that it was felt necessary to give him a helper. So, within twelve months or so of taking mourners' names in Norfolk churchyards, I found the portals of Buckingham Palace opening before me. But not very wide: the portal the Press use is actually an obscure side door leading not into luxurious State apartments but merely into an anonymous corridor along which lie the very business-like offices of the Press Officer and his staff. It was protected then not by a guardsman in a busby nor by a cavalryman with a drawn sword, but by a discreet figure clad in a sort of Government-surplus Civil Defence uniform of navy-blue blouse and trousers with only a little red crown on the pocket to distinguish it from the gear my father wore as an ARP warden.

Nevertheless, the glow of driving into that courtyard for the first time in my office Morris Minor, the nudges the tourists gave each other outside the gates as the policeman waved me through, the stroll across that immaculate gravel to the little side door, and then in due course the nonchalant drive out again, with perhaps a majestic nod to the small boys with their heads stuck in the railings – this was all sheer magic to the ex-star of the Dereham Players. I was also allowed to telephone the Palace, on a secret telephone number known only to every cub reporter in Fleet Street. This was only for making routine enquiries of the Press Office, but it still proved effective in the middle of a dinner party to rise with a faintly distracted air and murmur, 'I just have to telephone Buck House'. If people thought I was kidding, they could always hear the suave voice on the switchboard say 'Buckingham Palace'.

The main object of the appointment, though, was to relieve Godfrey of some of the lesser engagements and to lend a hand occasionally with the radio commentaries on big State occasions, notably the visits by foreign heads of State. These visits used to follow a fairly regular pattern, and I believe still do, though the BBC takes rather less notice of them now; when you have described one royal arrival you have just about described them all, apart from altering the names, the colours of the dresses and the degree of dampness of the weather, which on such occasions generally ranges from a gentle drizzle to a full-scale cloudburst.

The procedure was usually for the distinguished visitor to be set down at Gatwick Airport, largely because Gatwick used to be pretty quiet in the winter and no doubt they were glad to have somebody coming through. There the visitors boarded a Southern Region train for Victoria, where British Rail, mindful of the honour being done them, quite often swept the appropriate platform. The welcoming ceremony then took place on that platform, which always seemed a very sensible arrangement since the roof of Victoria Station did at least provide some protection from the appalling weather which so often accompanied the Queen at these times. Alas, it was impractical for the visitor to spend his entire stay in Victoria Station, and soon he had to emerge into the British climate.

The side exit was used, because at the main exit this would cause hold-ups in the traffic, and taxi drivers might be liable to shout things. Outside in the little courtyard by the Continental booking office was always the guard of honour, which had probably been standing there since about last Tuesday fortnight because the Army likes to have things ready on such occasions. It was then the duty of the visitor to inspect these three rows of saturated soldiery, and it was the practice of the officer in command to follow half a pace behind, bearing a drawn sword. It often struck me that a drawn umbrella might have been more useful, but as I understood it the sword was to ensure that the guest did not cheat and miss a row in order to get back under cover.

His ordeal, however, was not yet over, since they then brought round an open carriage to take him by the scenic route from Victoria Station to the Palace, These processions rarely attract large crowds today – why stand about in the rain when the whole thing will be on television tonight? – but fifteen years ago the route was generally well lined with holidaymakers and tourists, as well as a fair sprinkling of infuriated motorists whose cars had been caught in the enormous traffic jams that a royal procession inevitably involved. Still, they were quite often waving as well, even if the fists were slightly clenched.

The main commentary point was at the last stage of the drive, to cover the arrival at the Palace. It was situated in rather a conspicuous position, on that splendid circular edifice which stands just outside the gates with Queen Victoria esconced upon it, gloomily surveying the traffic in the Mall. I suppose it must have been some enterprising BBC engineer, driving past the Victoria Memorial one day, who realised what a splendid view she must have of all these processions, from the moment when the first horses came through Admiralty Arch until the last ones disappeared into the central Palace courtyard. Forthwith he converted Queen Victoria into an Outside Broadcasts Point, and if ever you feel moved to climb the Victoria Memorial today, you should still discover, sunk in the stonework, a trapdoor. Beneath it lie all manner of wires and plugs and sockets. You merely plug a microphone into one of these sockets, press a button, turn a switch, and you can address the nation, all through the courtesy of Queen Victoria.

There was not much actual training attached to becoming Number Two on the Royals; it was largely a matter of calling everybody 'Sir' or 'Ma'am' and keeping the head slightly bowed.

At least they allowed me one practice run on the Victoria Memorial before letting me loose on the real thing. It so happened that we were to have a State Visit by the King and Queen of Thailand, and four of us embryo commentators were detailed to take our tape-recorders onto the Memorial and record a trial commentary as the procession went by. First, of course, we did our research. We found out without too much difficulty where Thailand was, but when we discovered the name of the King of Thailand, warning bells began to ring, because his name was Bhumibol, which for an English tongue is difficult to pronounce with any sort of dignity. So we hastened off to an invaluable department of the BBC called the Pronunciation Unit (who get very irritated if you call them the Pron*ou*nciation Unit, as so many people do) and we asked for their guidance. 'Foomifol,' they said, to our considerable relief, and we went around practising 'Foomifol' under our breath, while passers-by eyed us nervously. The name of the Queen of Thailand seemed equally hazardous, so we returned in haste to the Pronunciation Unit.

'How do you pronounce "Sirikit"?' we asked.

'It is pronounced "Sirikit",' they replied coldly, and shut the door behind us.

Now fully briefed, we set off for the Victoria Memorial, to find of course that it was pouring with rain and that this noble pile offered no protection from it at all. However, in our group was Corbet Woodall, newly arrived at the BBC. Presumably he aspired like us to being a commentator, but he got so wet that day it may have decided him to become a newsreader instead. Corbet is, I believe, an Old Etonian; at any rate he invariably carried an umbrella, the only one in our number to do so on this occasion. The four of us crowded beneath it, back to back in a tight little circle, awaiting the arrival of the procession. This had the disadvantage that while the two of us facing outwards had a splendid view of the proceedings, the two facing inwards could see only the Victoria Memorial. We held an ad hoc committee meeting, as is the custom in the BBC in times of crisis, and we decided that the only fair thing to do, to give each of us an equal chance, was for all four of us to revolve.

When the procession went by we draped our tape recorders from our shoulders, held our microphones to our lips, Corbet held aloft the umbrella, and we revolved, commentating throughout.

C

One of the first impressions gained by the King and Queen of Thailand of the British way of life was this bizarre quartet on the Victoria Memorial, revolving beneath that invaluable umbrella. Still, they were extremely civil, and waved to us as they drove by. The four of us waved back as we revolved. Many years later the Magic Roundabout was to provide much the same effect.

We returned to the office with our tapes and played them over. Terrible, they said, but we don't have anyone else. In due course I was assigned my first 'live' commentary from the Memorial. President de Gaulle was to visit us, and a firework display was to be held in St James's Park. The President and the Queen would watch the display from that famous Palace balcony, and I was detailed to provide a two-minute description of the scene for the old Home Service. Some days before the display I wrote out my spontaneous commentary and learned it by heart. Godfrey always advised me that so long as you had a good opening line and a good payoff, nobody would ever remember what you said in between, but this was my first attempt and I played it safe.

On the great night I climbed onto the Memorial with a Royal Producer (our Royal Producers do not actually wear crowns, they just look as if they ought to), and together we opened that secret trapdoor, plugged in the microphone and the headphones and the portable telephone, and waited. At ten o'clock we heard the pips and that calm, utterly confident voice from the studio saying: 'Now we are going over to the Victoria Memorial for a description of the wonderful firework display in honour of President de Gaulle which is now in progress in St James's Park.' The Royal Producer did a little royal producing. He tapped me on the shoulder, smiled encouragingly, and said 'Go!'

Alas, there were nothing for me to 'go' about. Perhaps they had had a late dinner, or the speeches had gone on too long, or perhaps they couldn't find the matches, but there was still no sign of the wretched firework display. Nobody was on the balcony, the whole park was still plunged in darkness, there was not a sound or a movement anywhere. I had two minutes to describe the scene.

It may seem a simple task to talk about nothing for two minutes. Many people, given a drink or two, can talk about nothing for hours and hours. But it can be more tricky if you have a 'live' microphone before you and a few hundred thousand people at the other end. It would have presented no problems for Godfrey, who could develop a simple 'Good morning' into a

54

twenty-minute feature, nor for Audrey Russell, who once spent thirty-seven minutes describing seagulls at Tower Pier while Princess Margaret's wedding procession was held up in the City. But I had never attempted such a feat myself, and those two minutes seemed to stretch away into infinity. In my near-panic I remembered a Golden Rule the BBC gives you for such circumstances. Describe, they say, whatever you can see. I peered around this pitch-dark park, searching for inspiration. I could just make out a couple in some nearby bushes but thought it would be as well not to describe them. The only other visible feature was a small pond, on which floated three assorted ducks, and with the thought of Audrey's gallant performance to encourage me, I went about describing each individual duck.

By the end of a minute and a half I had said all there was to say about ducks, but at least there were only thirty seconds to go and I felt reasonably confident that, like any other Englishman, I could probably talk about the weather for thirty seconds. It was just about then that they let off the first firework. Unfortunately nobody had warned me that this first firework would be an enormous rocket, nor that it would go off from a shrub some three feet from the Victoria Memorial. I recall I was laboriously describing the lampposts at the time. 'Little pools of light,' I was saying, 'gleaming along the broad white ribbon of the Mall . . .' WHOOSH!

The Memorial was shrouded in a cloud of green smoke, and such was the unexpectedness, the closeness, the sheer volume of the explosion, that my thin veneer of BBC training vanished in a second. '*Yarr!*' I cried, giving a mighty start, and the microphone was jerked right out of the trapdoor. Silence fell over the nation's loudspeakers.

After the briefest of pauses, the continuity announcer came to the rescue. I heard a rather pained voice come over the air from Broadcasting House, one of our special, BBC, pained voices. 'We seem to have lost contact with the Victoria Memorial,' it said. 'I will play you a gramophone record. That, I knew, was about as low as you can get in the BBC. If they start playing gramophone records while you are supposed to be talking, you know you have hit rock bottom. Certainly that Royal Producer has never really looked me in the eye since. Somehow I survived, but they never let me loose on the Victoria Memorial again.

The royal engagements continued however: the Queen

distributing the Maundy money in Rochester Cathedral, Prince Philip presenting awards at the Design Centre, the Queen Mother visiting the Television Centre, Princess Margaret still opening garages, the delectable Princess Alexandra (I swear she used to wink at the pressmen during the more pompous of the speeches) opening an old people's centre at Southgate and school buildings in Winchmore Hill. At last, in April 1961, I was granted a little fruit-cake to add to all that royal bread and butter; I covered the Queen Mother's State Visit to Tunisia, followed immediately by the Queen's royal tour of Italy.

Tunisia at that time was not an ideal venue for one's first overseas assignment. To start with, most of the people there had an irritating habit of speaking only French, and what had sounded most convincing in my School Certificate oral apparently made no sense at all to the Tunisians. The food seemed to be mostly camel meat and sheep's eyes, much appreciated by the locals but a little indigestible for an inexperienced English stomach. Strange insects roamed the corridors, doubtless quite harmless but of uncommonly ferocious appearance. And I had no idea how to deal with enthusiastic Arabs offering me the services of their equally enthusiastic sisters. Happily I was taken under the wing of the BBC's man in Tunis, Freddie Matthews, a Waugh-type figure who in the heat of the day trod the streets of the city and penetrated the seamiest of the souks clad in a blue pinstripe suit and an ancient Homburg hat, plentifully sprinkled with an equal mixture of sand and cigarette ash. With his help I located the British Ambassador and the State Press Office (the basic starting points for any Royal Tour), obtained my various credentials inscribed in French and Arabic, and found the local radio station from which I would send my despatches back to London. I even learned the appropriate rejoinder for those importunate Arabs. If I had a problem I had only to spot that Homburg hat bobbing among the burnouses, and the problem soon melted away.

The stiff white envelopes began to appear in my hotel pigeonhole. Her Britannic Majesty's Ambassador was anxious for the honour of my company at a reception for the Queen Mother; the Director of Protocol prayed Monsieur Timpson John BBC to assist at the President's reception for Sa Majesté La Reine Mère Elizabeth at the Palace of the Republic ('Tenue: Cravate noire'); and in due course I dined with La Reine Mère

Elizabeth in Kairouan, Artichauts de Chbika, Couscous de Elass and all. It was my first experience of international good living at regal level, and although the couscous laid me low for twenty-four hours, it was not a bad introduction to the circuit.

The Queen Mother was magnificent throughout. It is no secret that among newsmen she is the favourite 'Royal', always ready to pause for a photograph, always having a word and a smile when they are needed most. My lasting memory of that tour was one of our lunatic dashes through the desert, with police outriders scattering all obstacles from our path – camels, sheep, stray Tunisians – and in the midst of this great cloud of sand the Queen Mother beaming happily through the car window as dust-covered children waved Union Jacks at her from the roadside. I have seen that beam in Croydon and Poplar and Penge; it captivated them equally in Hammamet and Sousse.

Thanks to Freddie Matthews and the pills supplied by the BBC doctor I came through my first royal tour without publicly disgracing myself, and flew on with renewed confidence to Italy. I write of these flights now with a certain nonchalance, but in 1961 it was still an adventure to find one's way to the right airport, let alone to the right plane, to negotiate the passport control and the Customs (how do you say 'Midget' in French?) and to quaff a duty-free Scotch at thirty thousand feet. It was also a terribly lonely affair, being thrown among strangers in strange surroundings, overtipping porters and being rooked by taxi-drivers. The real enjoyment of those early trips was not the travelling itself but the bragging about it afterwards. Later, when I went abroad for television news with a camera team to provide company and guidance, the journeys became more tolerable, but I still subscribe to Alistair Cooke's opinion that flying is ninety-five per cent boredom and five per cent panic. Being cooped up for hours like a battery hen, strapped to the seat while they stuff you with plastic food, is a pretty uncivilised way of getting from here to there.

The Italian tour was one of those unrestful affairs where the Queen spent only a day in each centre and life developed into a mad scramble of planes and trains and taxis, of trying to find local studios and, having found them, of trying to explain that I needed a line to London and could they cut this tape to two-minutes-thirty. The tour started in Sardinia, crossed to Naples and Rome, then to Ancona and north to Venice and inland to

Florence and Milan. I should have benefited from visiting such showplaces, but I was so worried about meeting circuit times and catching flights and deciphering Italian railway timetables that it all passed in something of a blur. I paced St Mark's Square, thinking only about the expiring batteries in my tape-recorder; I took a gondola up the Grand Canal, anxious only to reach the station in time for my train; I viewed the wonders of Florentine art, wishing only that I knew the Italian for 'Do you stock typewriter ribbons?'

There were consolations, and moments to remember. It was on this trip that I had my only experience of working alongside the legendary Richard Dimbleby, as *Britannia* sailed into Naples harbour. I was recording a two-minute commentary, Richard was describing it live for television, and while I had completed my modest contribution before the royal yacht had even reached the quayside, Richard was still going strong throughout the lengthy process of docking and tying up and lowering the gangway. There was one moment when I thought that Homer had nodded at last. Richard was describing the flags that bedecked the quayside and talked of them as the flags of the Commonwealth. With a certain guilty delight I noted that one of them bore the unmistakable crescent of Turkey. Before I had a moment to gloat, Richard had spotted the mistake. 'No,' he said, 'not the flags of the Commonwealth of course, but the flags of the NATO countries – there's Turkey, there's Italy . . .' and faultlessly, in the correct order, he rattled them off. I have read since of the arguments Richard Dimbleby had with the BBC, and I have read the criticisms of his sometimes pontifical style, but during that encounter in Naples I was deeply impressed by his complete mastery of his craft and the sheer professionalism of his work.

The other memorable acquaintance I made on that trip was Patrick Smith, the BBC's Rome correspondent and the epitome of a BBC foreign correspondent of the early nineteen-sixties. Patrick did not have to pursue information in Rome, for the whole of Rome came to him. I have sat beside him in some delightful open-air café while politicians and priests, generals and judges have come to his table with their problems, their rumours, their inside information. Alas, like a number of his post-war contemporaries in the foreign field, Patrick never really came to terms with television. I suspect he found it irksome to condense a thoughtful, beautifully polished report into a one-minute piece to the camera, with all the clauses reversed just to fit the pictures. He retired eventually to Switzerland, where I hope he continues to enjoy good health, good company and good English.

I returned home from my first 'short-term assignment abroad'– the promise of that original advertisement had materialised at last – to find my first major home assignment awaiting me. Godfrey had been taken ill and I was to replace him as a commentator at the wedding of the Duke of Kent and Katherine Worsley. I had a comparatively minor role, filling in the gaps between Audrey Russell and the other veterans, but it still involved carrying six different kinds of passes, signed by everyone from the Chief Constable to the local manager of British Railways, and mastering eight pages of ceremonial from the arrival of the first guests at York Minster to the departure of the couple five hours later.

It all went magnificently, as these great royal occasions always do, but the moment I remember most clearly came not from the ceremony, nor during the sumptuous reception that followed, but in a chat I had early that morning with a little Yorkshire lad in the grounds of the Minster, before the crowds had gathered and the excitement had all begun. He was musing quietly on one of the seats, and I asked him, just to be sociable, whether he knew what was due to happen there later that day.

'Ay, there's a wedding,' he replied. 'It's our Miss Worsley, but I don't know who t'man is.'

Which, I felt, put royal weddings in perspective, and Number Two on the Royals firmly in his place.

Chapter Seven

Over the next eighteen months my royal engagements gathered momentum, with Godfrey still out of action for long periods. (He sent me a card from hospital after the York Minster commentary, just saying 'Well done!' – a very typical gesture.) I endured a week of bagpipes and baps on the annual Royal Visit to Scotland, pursued them to Plymouth to join the good burghers in making hay on the Hoe, and escorted them to East Anglia to marvel at the button-boy balancing on the mast-top of HMS Ganges.

One particular excursion stood out, the Queen Mother's visit to Merchant Taylors' School for its quatercentenary celebrations. There was a certain gratification in walking through those familiar classrooms in such distinguished company, albeit several paces to the rear. It so happened that thirteen years later the Queen Mother was there again, to open a new music and science block, and on that occasion I was not a BBC 'observer' but a guest of the School, one of the fortunate ones to be presented. It was strange, after watching so many other formal presentations over the years, to be directly involved myself; the stage fright is just as severe, but the Queen Mother's interest in my modest activities was as convincing as if I had never seen her going through this procedure so many times before. Indeed, it is only after a year or so of covering these repetitive royal engagements that you appreciate the job which the 'royals' do, and the patience and thoroughness with which they do it. Through all those hours of shaking hands, listening to speeches, receiving bouquets, handing out awards, planting trees, cutting tapes, turning keys and opening valves, they still manage to be civil to total strangers. Every day they pack up their speeches in their glass-topped Rolls and smile, smile, smile.

It became routine enough just to watch this endless succession of ceremonies, let alone take part in them, but at the beginning of 1963 came the reward for those months on the regal rounds. It was no reward for the 'royals' themselves, who were to work harder than ever, but for me it was a splendid break from sipping sherry in Stevenage and taking tea in Thame. In the first week of February I took off for Auckland for the royal tour of New Zealand and Australia.

The winter of 1963 was a particularly bitter one in Britain, with temperatures well below zero and snow and ice covering the country. It was in fact an excellent period to spend in the Antipodes, but that was little consolation for Pat and Jeremy, who were of course left behind. By now we were living in a pleasant semi-detached in Croxley Green, just within the twenty-mile radius from Broadcasting House that was compulsory in those days for BBC reporters. Jeremy was six and growing up fast, and although we had many good friends in the area who were always on hand when needed, the royal tour unfortunately coincided with the expected arrival of our second baby; it was due in March, when I would be eleven thousand miles away, somewhere between Canberra and Brisbane. If I had been warned about the tour a little earlier, perhaps we could have planned things more conveniently – I suppose somebody must warn Prince Philip, but nobody told me. At this stage it seemed a little optimistic to suggest that they postpone the tour, so we had to resign ourselves to a rather unsatisfactory situation, which actually turned out even less fortunately than we had expected. Pat went down with 'flu, Jeremy got bronchitis, and the baby arrived three weeks early, mercifully fit but underweight.

I was ignorant of these worries at the time. A BBC cable reached me at 1.30 in the morning in an Adelaide hotel; 'Son arrived 0930 today, weight not known' – I suspect it was, but they tactfully omitted it – 'both doing well, many congratulations.' Although Adelaide is not the most festive or friendly of Australian cities (where else in that convivial country would a cameraman be refused breakfast in a hotel dining room for failing to wear a tie?), we managed to down a fair number of Fosters before dawn broke.

We should have given the baby a good Australian name, to establish that it was born while Daddy was in Australia with the Queen. If it had been a girl we might indeed have named her Adelaide, or perhaps Alice Springs Timpson, which has a sort of ring about it. It turned out to be a boy, though, which might have tempted me had I been in Sydney at the time, but we eventually settled for Nicholas, which had no Antipodean significance at all.

The flight out should have been a memorable one, but in those affluent days BBC reporters travelled first-class, up front with the free drinks trolley This turned out to be just as well, since we ran into thick fog which forced us to divert from New York to Boston, with a consequent six-hour delay, and some appalling electrical storms accompanied us right across America. In my euphoric condition I quite enjoyed the pyrotechnics all around us; without the moral support of that trolley I would have been quite terrified.

So many books have been written about the royal side of royal tours that to add even a single chapter would be superfluous. Godfrey, for example, used to produce every year a *Royalty Annual*, a sort of regal equivalent of those old Pip, Squeak and Wilfred books, with illustrated stories of the royal progresses, handshake by handshake. I still have the official commemorative volume the Australians issued after the tour, a hundred glossy pages recreating, says the foreword, Her Majesty's journey in all its most splendid and stirring moments. So there is no need for me to recall, for instance, the splendid and stirring moments when the guests at a Sydney garden party were repeatedly warned over the loudspeakers not to grasp the Queen's hand too tightly when they were presented (and with the muscles on some of those Australian matrons, the warning was not given lightly); or when a surf carnival at Coolangatta was held in a torrential downpour which nearly led to the canvas canopy over the royal dais collapsing under the weight of water and providing the one picture the cameramen had come ten thousand miles for; or when a trotting meeting in Wellington continued so late that we prayed the wretched horses would all break into a gallop and get it over.

No need, as I say, to record these more public moments, which are amply chronicled, if rather more soberly, elsewhere. Far less has been written about the bizarre events which go on behind the scenes, away from all the handshakes and the bouquets, among the correspondents who cover the royal tours. They are on the whole an irreverent, bawdy bunch, however impressive they may look at the rear of the processions, and eight weeks in their company was a revelation and a delight. There were about seventy of us in the Press party, from veterans like Rene MacColl of the *Daily Express* and Vincent Mulchrone of the *Daily Mail*, right down to the new boys like me. One of our number was Leslie Thomas, working at that time for the London *Evening*

News, and later to achieve world fame as author of *The Virgin Soldiers* and all its successors. Leslie went down with appendicitis in Sydney and had to drop out of the party, which I suspect disappointed him not at all. Eulogising over royal garden parties and the sun shining on the soldiery was not really his natural style.

The actual reporting of a royal tour, incidentally, is about the easiest part of the job. We had a wealth of background information presented to us in our smart black brief-cases with the big royal crest (most useful if held ostentatiously when returning home through Customs), and our task was merely to select which nuggets of knowledge we favoured most. It might be the street decorations in Melbourne (pale blue and white, slashed with scarlet and gold) or the number of sheep per acre in New Zealand (there are forty-eight million sheep in a total area of 103,416 square miles; you can work it out from there).

The really difficult part of covering this tour, I found, was simply keeping up. It was not such a problem during the day. We were all allocated seats in the great procession of cars that followed the Queen around the countryside, although with the large numbers involved, and my own status being slightly lower than fourth footman, it was touch and go in the early stages whether I would be allowed a seat at all. There was some rather disturbing talk at one point about a bicycle, but eventually they gave me a seat right at the rear of the cavalcade, in about Car 45. We used to have problems in Car 45, because whenever this enormous procession pulled up, say in the centre of Auckland, Car 45 still seemed to be several miles up the coast, somewhere the far side of Mount Maunganui, with no indication of what might be happening up at the front. Whenever we stopped, all of us third-eleven chaps at the back had to leap out of our cars and dash to the head of the column to see where we were. Quite often we discovered it was merely the traffic lights against us, so we all had to dash back again. It was a very unrestful way of seeing the world.

At least we had seats, even though the seats were a little distant from the action, and it was quite entertaining to hear the speculation among the crowd as we brought up the rear of the long line of limousines. Plain-clothes men was the most popular theory, which I encouraged by keeping my right hand under my left armpit and assuming a menacing scowl. Some of the more

63

The royal procession arriving at Victoria Park, Adelaide. The BBC's Special Correspondent is not yet in sight, since Car 45 is probably just leaving Melbourne.

romantic of the onlookers imagined us to be gentlemen-in-waiting, poised to fling our raincoats over obtrusive puddles or to crouch before the Royal personage to provide a mounting-block onto a passing horse. The most penetrating analysis came from a small boy in Wellington, who ran alongside my car for a considerable distance, announcing to the crowd at the top of his voice, 'Here comes Fishface'.

It was the nights which provided the real problems. Each night during our fortnight in New Zealand the Queen would board the royal yacht to sail round the coast for the next day's engagements. The BBC did not run to a yacht, and we had to rely on whatever forms of transport were provided by the New Zealand government. We could not cheat and make our departure ahead of the Queen, lest some frightful disaster struck as she went up the gangway. Nor could we afford to arrive after her, in case some other disaster occurred as she came down again. So our nights were spent leapfrogging *Britannia* round the coast of New Zealand, generally in aeroplanes, sometimes in cars, once – the most memorable leap of all – in a train. It was a special train laid on to take the Press from Waitangi, up in the tranquil Bay of Islands, the place where the Maoris signed a treaty with the British in 1840 (copiously described in our official handouts), down to Auckland (population 466,300, average annual rainfall forty-nine inches – those handouts omitted nothing). It was only 150 miles or so, but to allow us a little sleep on the way, the train was to take some six hours to cover them.

I shared a compartment with a senior representative of the New Zealand Broadcasting Corporation, who by virtue of his rank had first choice of bunks and unwisely selected the lower. We bade each other good night and turned in, while the train headed gently south. But not gently enough. The track we were running on seemed to have warped in the sun, and after half an hour or so we were subjected to a shuddering and shaking so violent that I was propelled from my bunk into the arms of the senior representative of the NZBC. This was a most embarrassing situation, since not only does the BBC strongly disapprove of this sort of thing, but our difference in status was so substantial that technically I should not even have spoken to the man, let alone fallen on top of him. All communications, say staff regulations, should be addressed to such executives through their personal secretaries and his, alas, was not there. I could only climb off this unfortunate fellow, apologise on behalf of the Corporation for my unseemly conduct, and struggle back on to my bunk.

The track did not improve. More jolts and shudders came throughout the journey, and all down the train one could hear the thuds and expletives of plummeting pressmen. I learned afterwards that it was great fun in some of the more assorted compartments, but it did me no good at all. I arrived in Auckland sleepless, shaken and sour, but at least we were greeted with some encouraging news. That evening we were to go on board *Britannia* to be presented to the Queen, a pleasant privilege accorded to the Press at the beginning of major tours and designed, as one veteran solemnly advised me, to assist newcomers like myself to recognise Her Majesty when we attended the functions that followed.

After a comparatively quiet day, therefore – just the speeches of welcome at Princes Wharf, the ceremonial drive to a public welcome where the Queen drove at walking pace through thousands of Aucklanders, another twelve-mile drive back to the quayside through apparently every street in the town, another drive after lunch to the Tamaki Yacht Club for a royal regatta, and then the return drive along a totally different route to give every resident a close-up view without budging from his front gate – as I say, after a comparatively quiet day on this crowded tour the Queen prepared to receive us on board the royal yacht.

As we reached the deck I had the privilege of enjoying my only conversation ever with Prince Philip. He was awaiting us at the top of the gangway (though not actually taking the tickets), and when it came to my turn he enquired very civilly, 'Who are you?'

'I am Timpson, sir,' I revealed, 'of the BBC.'

There was a long, pregnant pause, one of those pauses where your whole past life flashes before you. Then he spoke.

'Oh,' said the Duke, and moved on.

It may not have been a very long conversation, but I felt it came from the heart. I cherish it to this day.

The reception itself was one of those well ordered affairs where the drinks seem to get progressively weaker as the evening goes on, and where the Queen's perambulations were planned so precisely that each group was advised a few seconds before her imminent arrival, and given a pretty clear indication of how long she intended to stay. I assumed at the time that all royal socialising was planned as precisely as this, with a floorplan, a set of compasses and a stopwatch. It was only years afterwards, when Pat and I had the good fortune to attend a more informal, late night reception at the Palace (with only 300 guests present, compared with the 7,000 at a garden party, and thus a fairly intimate affair), that we found the Queen and indeed all the 'royals' circulating freely like any other hosts, unfettered by the necessity of meeting the maximum number of people in the minimum amount of time.

My group at the Auckland reception included Ronnie Read, the veteran ITN cameraman, who had just returned from the Antarctic and was wearing a miniature penguin on his tie-clip. This could hardly fail to catch the royal eye, and the conversation during our statutory three minutes was confined to sub-zero topics, with my own contributions limited to appreciative nods and the occasional genteel chuckle. My carefully rehearsed observations about the weather, the state of the tide, and the excellent condition of the yacht's paintwork, turned out not to be required.

Even the best planned parties can have their unexpected moments, and during the course of this one the *Daily Mirror* cameraman, another old hand called Freddie Reed, had the misfortune to drop his glass not far from the Queen's feet. At the crash of breaking glass the gathering fell suddenly silent, and my fevered imagination pictured the scenes to come – Freddie taken away in irons, the Beefeaters awaiting him at Traitor's Gate, a lifetime of incarceration in the Tower. Actually it all passed off rather well. I had underestimated the forward planning of the Court officials, for no sooner had the glass fallen to the deck than a door opened near Her Majesty and a sailor appeared bearing a dustpan and brush. It was like a cuckoo popping out of a clock, so sudden and immediate was his arrival. No doubt the crew had been warned that the Press were on board, and were prepared for all manner of hooliganism. The sailor sank to his knees, brushed up the broken glass, and mopped the deck with an immaculate white cloth. Throughout this performance, to my immense admiration, the Queen continued to chat to those about her, completely ignoring the activity around her feet. It was a masterly handling of a rather embarrassing situation.

That same evening there was a curious sequel to this incident, again involving the unfortunate Freddie. The Press party had assembled outside St James's Theatre in Auckland for a royal

67

opera performance staged by the New Zealand Opera Company, whose chairman was a Mr Turnovsky (how I hankered to include that name in a despatch). The cameramen were ranged up the steps to the entrance, with Freddie well to the fore. As the Queen came level with him, looking magnificent under the arc lights in evening dress and decorations and jewels, he pressed his camera button – and the flashbulb exploded. Once again the debris was scattered around him, and the rest of us, to a man, turned to see if that sailor would appear again with his dustpan and brush. But this time no cuckoo clock opened. Instead the Queen herself paused beside him, and the whole procession came to a halt. The great crowd outside the theatre fell silent as she turned to the hapless Freddie.

'Mr Reed,' she said – and the whole of Auckland held its breath – 'Mr Reed, it's just not your night!' And with a big smile she sailed on into the theatre.

I can almost claim, on behalf of the Press party, that I played a modest role in averting a possible diplomatic crisis during the Queensland section of the tour. It occurred at a koala bear sanctuary just outside Brisbane, where the little chaps live under Government protection. The sanctuary consisted of rows and rows of eucalyptus trees, and wrapped around each tree was a koala bear, with his little flattened nose and his big sad eyes – a natural consequence, it was explained to me, of spending one's life wrapped around a gumtree. The Press arrived ahead of the royal party and while we waited the warden suggested we might like to be photographed with a koala. It seemed useful evidence that we really were in Australia and not sending bogus despatches from Earls Court, so we gratefully agreed. 'Get Fred!' cried the warden, and Fred was unwound from his gumtree. He was a specially photogenic koala, not too inclined to bite, and constantly posing with visiting dignitaries, so that the fur on his back had worn patches from the patting of numberless nervous hands.

Each one of us in turn held out our hands for Fred, and he sat there looking soulful while each photograph was taken. By the time it came to my turn it was about the sixty-second photograph, and Fred had been away from his gumtree too long. As he was placed in my hands those big sad eyes became sadder than ever, and he could contain himself no longer. It proved to be one of the highlights of the tour for my colleagues, and that shirt could never be worn again, but I have often consoled myself with this thought. Only a few minutes later the Queen arrived at the sanctuary, and she too was invited to be photographed with Fred. The Press watched eagerly but on this occasion Fred behaved with perfect decorum. But supposing, I have often asked myself,

The BBC's Deputy Court Correspondent and friend, during the 1963 Royal tour of Australia. The smile faded a few seconds later, when Fred the Koala proved that he was some way from being fully house-trained.

supposing not I but the Queen had been number sixty-two. Empires have foundered on less. And I am proud to have borne on her behalf some of the heat and burden of that day.

This was not our only unlikely encouter with Australian fauna. We came upon other varieties, in most unexpected circumstances, at the top of the Snowy Mountains. The Queen was spending four days touring the remarkable hydro-electric complex up among the peaks of the Snowy, where they were driving a hundred miles of tunnels through the mountains to divert the waters of the Snowy River from the well-irrigated side of the range to the barren lands on the other, and building ten entire power stations inside the mountains to tap the hydro-electric power as the water flowed through. It was an impressive four days, driving up precarious tracks with a sheer drop beside us, the turnings so sharp that our coach had to manoeuvre back and forth to negotiate them, the rear frequently projecting over the precipice. The most memorable incident occurred on Lake Eucumbene, the great artificial lake which had been created among the actual mountain peaks.

The Queen was to sail across this lake, and at the usual Press briefing on the previous evening the Australians advised us that when she sailed past a certain island, at 4 pm precisely, she would be able to observe on the beach an emu and a wallaby. There would be a pause for her to take photographs before the launch proceeded on its way. I for one was tremendously impressed. How could they know with such certainty, I wondered, that at 4 pm precisely there would emerge onto the beach an emu and a wallaby? The event had a touch of the supernatural about it, and was definitely not to be missed. We boarded the Press launch with an unusual sense of expectation that afternoon, and set off behind the royal launch across the lake. Sure enough, as we drew level with the island at 4 pm precisely, there on the beach were the emu and wallaby. The Queen took photographs of them, the cameramen took photographs of the Queen taking photographs of them, and the Duke doubtless took photographs of the cameramen.

I felt impelled to probe into the background of this faunal fantasy, and the story they told me was so unbelievable it might almost be true. It did at least provide an example of the planning that goes into a Royal Tour. Apparently the organisers felt it would be a happy thought if the Queen could see some of

Australia's most famous indigenous species in their natural habitat. Some weeks before the tour, therefore, they acquired from Sydney Zoo an emu and a wallaby and transported them up the mountains to Lake Eucumbene. Each day during the weeks that followed, some devoted soul visited the island at 4 pm precisely and scattered along the beach various comestibles of particular appeal to the two guests. Of course it eventually dawned on the emu and wallaby that it was a sound move to appear on that beach round about four o'clock each afternoon, and they appeared right on time for the Queen's visit. Although that was back in 1963, will there emerge from out of those bushes, at four o'clock precisely this afternoon, an ageing emu and a geriatric wallaby?

From the Snowy Mountains we headed for the Outback, and after a few days there we could understand why they had it out the back – nobody could possibly want it round the front. Nevertheless we all said how splendid it was, because it is politic to say everything in Australia is splendid when speaking to Australians, and perhaps as a reward for our good behaviour they arranged a sea cruise for the last lap of the tour from Darwin to Perth. They put the Press on board the motor vessel *Koolama* for the three-day voyage round the coast of Western Australia. It looked like a pleasant change from the dusty car rides and cramped flights, and we boarded the *Koolama* with considerable enthusiasm. As we went on board each one of us was handed a paper parcel, a gift from the Federal Government of Australia. Eagerly we tore off the wrappings. Each of us had the same present – a packet of washing powder.

Here indeed was an illustration of the practical and down-to-earth way in which Australians go about organising royal tours, for one of the problems of a travelling tour like this, where each night is spent in transit and each day in the royal cavalcade, is that wherever one goes they have a public holiday in honour of the Queen so everything shuts, including the laundries. Day after day we would arrive at a hotel at breakfast time, hand in our dirty washing, and have it handed back again because the laundry was on holiday. Night after night we would re-pack it, add that day's washing, and move on. In a climate where one can get through three or four shirts a day, even the miracle of drip-dry nylon cannot keep up the pace, and by the time we reached Darwin, after nearly eight weeks on the road, we had to grapple with extra carrier bags and cumbersome parcels to hold our backlog of laundry. I suspect it reached the stage there, where it is very hot indeed, that people began to notice when the Press got off the plane.

How extremely sensible, therefore, to give us this washing powder. Forthwith we set to over sinks and baths and buckets, and soon the good ship *Koolama* was festooned from bow to funnel to stern with a striking array of journalists' smalls. We were still decorated thus when the skipper cast off and we sailed out of harbour – as it happened, right past Her Majesty's Royal Yacht *Britannia*. The familiar phrase, 'dressing a ship overall', took on an entirely new meaning. Prince Philip, I think was most impressed. We thought we discerned him on the bridge, standing at the salute, so those of us with any clothes left to wear formed up on deck and saluted back. It may not have been up to Spithead standards, but I think Darwin will long remember the day when the British Press sailed for Perth and home. As we dipped over the horizon I wonder if they could hear us singing the chorus which was the anthem of the Press corps throughout the tour, and which still serves as a greeting if any of that 1963 contingent meet today:

> What a day this has been,
> We have just seen the Queen,
> For the hundred and fiftieth time . . .

Chapter Eight

In my eagerness to see the new addition to the family, now six weeks old, I returned home from Australia on a continuous flight in just over twenty-four hours, a pointless gesture since I then needed forty-eight hours' sleep to recover. Happily the illnesses had passed, Nicholas was prospering, and the only let-down came when I strolled into my local, a bronzed foreign correspondent back from the Antipodes, only to be asked whether I had enjoyed my holiday.

Apparently some of my despatches had been heard by somebody, and no majesté had been lèsed for my regal activities continued. Another royal wedding was coming up, and I joined the team at Westminster Abbey to watch Princess Alexandra plight her troth (on this occasion I think there were no winks for the Press). As far as newsmen are concerned the groom has proved as charming as his bride, and it was typical that when their first baby was born, Angus Ogilvy came out personally to tell those of us waiting outside, bearing a bottle of champagne for us to celebrate the news.

Then it was back to the Maundy money circuit with Tweedledum and Tweedledee, but with occasional dramas to break the routine. The most spectacular crime story of the decade broke for me at eight o'clock one morning, merely because I happened to live within reach of an obscure Buckinghamshire village called Cheddington. The office rang me with a report of a mail train being held up, and not believing a word of it I crawled out of bed and into the car, cursing my luck. There was an impromptu press conference going on at the station, and a police spokesman was being asked how much had been stolen. 'About a million and a half pounds,' he said, and we all smiled politely and invited him to pull the other one. Actually that was an underestimate, as anyone who recalls the Great Train Robbery will know. It was the start of some very dramatic dashing about in the peaceful countryside of Buckinghamshire and Bedfordshire in pursuit of false alarms and mythical leads.

By the time they caught up with the majority of the Great Train Robbers I had become involved in a totally different branch of BBC activity. At that time it was merely a pleasant break in the standard reporting duties, whether they were robberies or royals. As it turned out, it was a foretaste of the dawn patrol that was later to become an entire new way of life. In May 1964 I served my first month as a relief presenter on 'Today'.

The 'Today' routine was rather gentler in those days than it is now. Jack de Manio was its cornerstone, just as William Hardcastle was becoming the cornerstone of 'The World at One'. Like Bill, Jack did not present every programme, though I am sure the public had that impression and never noticed the shadowy substitutes who took his place. While Bill presented 'The World at One' three days a week, Jack presented 'Today' two months in three, and during that third month the BBC rounded up whatever local labour it could find to fill the gap. Although only one presenter handled a complete programme, it was a far less arduous task than under the present 'double-harness' arrangement. The programme contained mainly magazine items, with only a comparatively casual glance at the news of the day. It started later, at 7.15, and the second half was almost entirely a repeat of the first. It was not so much a programme, more a way of telling the time, and so long as we fulfilled that duty every three minutes or so, and sounded reasonably cheerful about it, the listeners did not seem to worry too much about what went on in between.

'Today' was produced by the same group that turned out the more stately prestige programme in the evening, 'Ten O'Clock', and our early-morning activities were not taken too seriously. Those were the days of eccentric octogenarians, prize pumpkins, and folk who ate light bulbs and spiders, with the occasional quotation from 'Peterborough' to fill up any gaps. The scripts were largely written by the production team, and the presenter needed to arrive only a few minutes before the programme (in Jack's case, only a few seconds on some mornings) to adjust the odd word. But this was my first experience of mass-audience live broadcasting, and I enjoyed it enormously. The first month proved a success with my masters, but although I filled in on a number of occasions after that, taking turns with Brian Johnston, Robert Hudson and Martin Muncaster during the months when Jack was away, it was to be another six years before the

74

changes which brought me permanently into the 'Today' team.

Meanwhile, once that first month was over, I dropped back into the comparative anonymity of the reporters' pool until my court duties took me abroad again, this time to Iceland. Of all my royal excursions this must have been the most unorthodox, and certainly the most uncomfortable. Prince Philip was making an official visit to Reykjavik, but being Prince Philip he was doing it the hard way, sailing there in *Britannia* in order to visit the British fishing fleet on the way. The BBC, no longer so indulgent over first-class fares, arranged a free passage for me on board the escorting frigate *Malcolm*, along with the 'royal' cameraman, Bernard Hesketh. Bernard and I had first met on the Australian tour, but as I had been concerned only with radio we had worked separately. The Iceland trip was the first of many that we made as a team, Bernard taking silent film, myself providing a tape-recorded commentary. We worked together in later years on less congenial assignments after we had both come off the royal rota, notably in Cyprus and the Lebanon, but none was quite such an endurance test as that voyage on board HMS *Malcolm*.

A frigate is not built for comfort at the best of times, and although this was midsummer, we spent most of the three-day journey in a force 9 gale. We slept, when sleep was possible, in a glorified cupboard in the hold, which we shared with a delightful Nigerian midshipman. It was known throughout the ship as the Kasbah. Mostly we sat jammed behind the wardroom table, clutching a succession of horse's necks. This is the admirable naval remedy for seasickness; it may not cure it, but at least it renders you insensible to it. It is a combination of brandy and ginger ale with a twist of lemon, preferably topped up with more brandy, and can be taken for any form of illness or depression with almost infallible success. Thanks to its miraculous powers we survived those three days, and under its influence we even braved the high seas in a Gemini – a sort of inflatable dinghy with an outboard motor – to board a trawler while the Duke was visiting the fleet. It was consoling to find that the trawlermen, who had endured the same foul weather, had adopted the same remedy, varying it occasionally with stiff measures of rum and whisky. This all led to a highly convivial party on board the trawler, in which the Duke may well have joined, though all I can recall of it was the generosity of the trawlermen and the all-pervading stench of fish. As I had fallen heavily into the scuppers at some stage of the party, this stench remained with me throughout the rest of the voyage, causing the Kasbah to be re-christened Macfisheries.

As we eventually neared the Icelandic coast, mercifully the weather cleared and we had a close-up view of that astonishing new addition to the North Sea charts, the newly arisen island of Surtsey, still covered in its pall of steam and smoke, its surface still too hot to walk on. It had appeared out of the sea only a week or two before, and it looked eerily like something on another planet, or perhaps how our planet will eventually look – smouldering, sombre, and very dead.

Our arrival in Reykjavik was a much gayer affair. In order to get us ashore ahead of the Duke, our naval friends supplied us with a Gemini and landed us just a few moments before the Duke's more dignified arrival by launch. In our weather-worn BBC Gannex coats we popped up on the red-carpeted quayside out of our little rubber dinghy, looking rather like illegal immigrants in search of Bradford. The welcoming dignitaries were a little shaken, but the crowd were absolutely delighted and applauded us madly as we stumbled ashore.

It was the start of an entertaining week in Iceland, visiting the geysers and the hot springs which supply Reykjavik with its central heating, and the great greenhouses scattered around the countryside where bananas and pineapples can grow inside the glass while outside the landscape is barren and bleak. Being midsummer there was no real darkness at night, and it was curious to emerge from a restaurant at midnight and walk back to the hotel in broad daylight. This was in fact how the night clubs effectively sobered up their clients when they wanted to close – they just drew back the curtains, and a romantic, cosy evening would end abruptly in bright sunshine. Very disconcerting for young couples, and I imagine engagements must be pretty rare in Iceland during the summer. However, when I celebrated my birthday in Reykjavik, the crew of *Malcolm* threw an excellent party with a whole cavalry charge of horse's necks, and the wardroom curtains stayed firmly drawn until a more civilised daybreak hour.

Two fete openings, a General Election, and another four weeks on 'Today' later, I was off with Bernard again on a very different State Visit, to Ethiopia and the Sudan. Although I was to cover other royal visits in later years, to Malta and Austria, this excursion to one of the lesser known corners of Africa was easily the most memorable. Ethiopia in particular provided some of the most bizarre moments I ever experienced on a royal tour.

All the panoply of a State Visit could not conceal the basic truths about Ethiopia. In the capital itself new luxury hotels soared above filthy mud huts. Around the elegant statues beggars sat in the gutters. The few main streets were reasonably paved, but the side roads were just rutted tracks. Outside the capital itself life was poverty-stricken and feudal. Everywhere one found disease. It was not by chance that the tourist maps of Addis Ababa listed not only the public monuments and the hotels but the VD clinics as well.

Out in more isolated areas, many of the old savage customs still survived. I had read before leaving home, for instance, that it had been the practice of victorious tribesmen to remove the more personal parts of their vanquished opponents and string them into necklaces for ceremonial occasions. Pat and I had chuckled over this, but it so happened that when my first tape from Ethiopia was broadcast back home they accidentally started playing it at double speed. My voice went up a couple of octaves, and Pat stopped chuckling.

That particular hazard never materialised, and indeed the Ethiopian officials made every effort to smooth the path of the British Press. It was not entirely their fault if arrangements sometimes deteriorated into farce, as was the case right at the start of the tour, when the Queen landed at Addis Ababa airport.

At the Press briefing the previous evening the British contingent, about twenty of us, had asked if we could leave the airport ahead of the royal procession, so that we could be present for the welcome in the city itself. It was agreed that we should have special transport for this purpose, and in the morning our special transport did indeed await us – a very elderly Green Line bus, pensioned off perhaps from the Reigate run and now patrolling the streets of Addis Ababa, with an enthusiastic Ethiopian at the wheel. This safely delivered us to the airport, and we were duly able to record the historic moment when the Queen first set foot on Ethiopian soil. The usual handshakes and speeches got under way, and we felt it reasonable to take the rest of the ceremony for granted, so we instructed our driver to head for town.

We only got as far as the airport gate. An Ethiopian sergeant, a magnificent figure of a man, stood before it and showed no inclination to move. We told him that we were the British Press and we had received permission to leave the airport ahead of the Queen. The sergeant told us in return that his orders were perfectly clear: nobody was allowed out of that gate ahead of Her Britannic Majesty. We raised our voices slightly and repeated our request. The sergeant raised his voice quite considerably, and told us to stay where we were. It looked like stalemate, but such setbacks are not enough to baulk a coachload of British journalists. It was René MacColl, I think, a man of great experience in such situations, who tapped our driver on the shoulder, tucked some notes in his top pocket, and told him to drive straight at the gate. Nothing could have delighted him more. An enormous grin came over his face and he crashed the gears into reverse.

'You wish me to ram the gate, sir?' he cried. 'I will back up a little and get a good run at it!'

And so he did, right across the tarmac into the heart of the welcoming ceremony beside the Queen's plane. There were the guard of honour, the band, the dignitaries, the Queen and the Emperor; and into the midst of them backed our ancient bus. There was the briefest pause as we ground to a halt and our driver got into bottom gear for the charge.

'Ready, gentlemen?' he shouted.

'Ready!' we cried. And off we hurtled towards the gate.

By this time the attention of the crowd was entirely devoted to the manoeuvres of our bus. Even the band faltered in mid-tune to watch our progress, and I rather suspect the Queen and the Emperor cast discreet glances in our direction too. The Ethiopian sergeant on the gate, a man of considerable personal courage, remained gallantly at his post until the bonnet of the bus was almost upon him. Finally, seeing the maniacal gleam in our driver's eye, he accepted the inevitable. He jumped aside, flung open the gate, and with tremendous dignity sprang to the salute and bellowed: 'British Press — hooray!'

Outside the gate thousands of people were lining the route, and all of them had been assured that the first person to emerge from that gate would be Her Majesty the Queen. When our old bus burst into view they very reasonably assumed that this must be an overseas version of the State Coach. Tremendous cheers greeted us on all sides. Children waved Union Jacks, men shouted, women wept. It was an amazing reception, and since it seemed a pity not to respond to all this enthusiasm, one of the girls in our party, Anne Sharpley, I think, of the *Evening Standard*, sat beside our lunatic driver and waved graciously as we thundered by. The rest of us bowed and smiled and left them guessing which one of us was the Duke. It was a riotous journey, and from then on a slightly hysterical atmosphere pervaded the Press party throughout the whole tour. Our only worry was that once we had passed by, the crowd might disperse before the real Queen arrived, but happily they stayed on and enjoyed two royal arrivals for the price of one.

The events that followed were liable to vary suddenly from the barbaric to the bizarre. The famous Imperial lions turned out to be elderly equivalents of Fred the Koala, permanently exhausted from posing for the cameras and reluctant even to get to their feet, let alone look noble. The Emperor presented a magnificent white stallion to the Queen, but unfortunately the Press bus went to the wrong royal palace, so we arrived too late for the ceremony. For the benefit of the cameramen, the Emperor and the Queen helpfully re-emerged from the palace, the horse re-emerged from the stable, and he presented it to her all over again.

We travelled the country in ancient Dakotas of the Imperial Ethiopian Air Force, landing in the more isolated areas on grass strips which the Air Force shared with the local sheep. If the sheep declined to vacate the runway we had to circle overhead until the station commander and the guard of honour had shooed them off. Communications were sometimes as unpredictable as the transport. In one little town the international Press corps descended on the local post office with their telex messages and wire-service photographs and colourful, action-packed reports, to find that the only link with the outside world was one man with a morse-tapper. Robert Hudson, from Outside Broadcasts, and I were entirely reliant on the facilities of Ethiopian radio, and were forced to remain incommunicado once we had left Addis Ababa until the final day when we reached their only other studio, in Asmara.

Yet there was a kind of rugged drama about the country, and a primitive dignity about its people, which in spite of all the ludicrous moments of the tour left me with a deep impression of a nation which has tremendous potential if only it can catch up with the rest of the world. The Emperor in his final years did what

79

he could, but there was too much corruption around him and the antiquated system of land tenure made it impossible to modernise the agriculture on which the economy depends. Looking back, the eventual coup seems inevitable, but Ethiopia's new rulers have yet to prove they can do any better.

Meanwhile the organisers of the Royal Tour did attempt to demonstrate how some ancient customs could be adapted for the twentieth century. They staged a 'gouks' match, where warriors gallop about in full war regalia, hurling spears at each other. Until quite recently, they assured us, these spears were the real thing, but when they began to run short of participants they gave them blunted tips. Even so it was a pretty terrifying display, especially as the Press had a place of honour right on the touchline and the warriors' aim was not always too accurate. Bob Hudson, who divided his time in those days between royal events and Test matches, tried recording a commentary on the match from what seemed a safe position at square leg, only to find spears flying past him from all directions, in a nightmare version of Lords on a bad day against the West Indies.

So we meandered through this astonishing country, sharing dormitories where no hotels existed and in one case, where no beds existed, sleeping in a bar. Cameramen sent off their film via Ethiopian Airlines, only to find on occasions that they got home before the film did, while reporters queued for the morse-tapper. I wrote a piece about the organisation and methods of the Ethiopian Civil Service which our foreign editor at the time, John Crawley, returned to me with the observation that had it been broadcast, Ethiopia would probably have severed diplomatic relations with us.

Finally we drove down from the mountains into Asmara, a city much modernised by the Italians. Here the authorities decided that as a farewell gesture at the airport, it would be a nice idea to scatter rose petals on the Queen's head from a passing aeroplane. Unfortunately they omitted to mention this to anyone beforehand, or perhaps some of the more experienced members of the Queen's entourage would have dissuaded them, since manifestly it was an operation fraught with hazards.

So indeed it turned out. As the Queen stood on the dais with the guard of honour before her, one of those now familiar Dakotas hove in sight just above the hedges, heading straight for the royal party. While the more nervous of us dived for cover, the

80

pilot's window opened and down came the rose petals – all over the guard of honour. As it turned out this was just as well, since the National Anthem was being played at the time, and this is not an ideal moment to drop rose petals over the royal person, but I shall long remember the vision of that guard of honour, enormous warriors clad in traditional robes and headdresses and bearing shields and spears, and now submerged under a fine layer of Ena Harkness – the first flower people in Ethiopia.

Meanwhile the pilot was so carried away with the excitement of the occasion that he hurled down at us not only the petals, but also the bags which had contained them. Had his aim been shrewder, we could have been singing the National Anthem to a sovereign with a sack over her head.

This event, and others like it, I recorded in an Ethiopian ode which I gather found its way into the Royal Household and was received not too unkindly. Its spirit was summed up in the opening verse:

> Hail to thee, Ethiopia,
> The country we all love so well,
> Where the people are charming,
> So polite, so disarming,
> But can they run tours? Can they hell!

The following week in the Sudan proved almost an anti-climax. Much of the administration was still based on British foundations, and only occasionally did we get a reminder of our earlier adventures. I was just in time, for instance, to prevent a Sudanese official with a limited knowledge of English Christian names from billeting René MacColl in the same bedroom as Anne Sharpley – I never discovered whether they were grateful or disappointed. But the only actual event of the four-day tour which really got out of hand was the great camel parade at El Obeid.

The idea was an impressive one. Forty thousand camels were to parade past the Queen, ridden by Dervishes equipped with swords, rifles, whips, and other standard Sudanese riding gear. The camels themselves behaved rather well, but the spectators were quite overcome by the spectacle and began surging towards the royal dais, which was already almost invisible in a cloud of white dust. The local constabulary lashed out indiscriminately, in what René later described in the *Express* as a 'head-conking, leg-slashing scrimmage', without the slightest effect. In the midst of this chaos I found myself next to a small table, which I mounted to avoid the worst of the crush, whereupon two small black babies were thrust into my arms by their terrified mother, to preserve them from being trampled by the crowd. I stood on my table, clutching these unfortunate infants and feeling like Son of Mother Courage, until order was eventually restored. The Queen, needless to say, remained entirely unperturbed, cool as ever in a nasturtium-tinted print dress and matching hat (I quote the *Express* again, which never misses such details), and not disconcerted even when presented with a baby gazelle, which is not the easiest gift to accept with dignity. What she did with the gazelle I never discovered, but at least I was able to dispose of the two babies, I hope to the same woman who gave them to me.

I did return from that tour with one memento which proved almost as embarrassing. It was an Ethiopian bird-charming flute, sold to me by a shrewd old con-man in Asmara, who assured me that it had the power to charm birds down from the trees. The flute had twin pipes and twin mouthpieces, and the theory was that if you blew down the right-hand pipe, the note so emitted would encourage the bird to lift its right leg. Similarly, a blast on the left pipe would set the left leg a-twitching. The coup de grâce, of course, was to blow down both pipes, thus causing the bird to lift both feet simultaneously and fall helpless to the ground.

A week or so after my return I was boasting about this remarkable acquisition, unaware that on that very day a certain golden eagle had escaped from London Zoo, and nobody could persuade it to return. The Editor happened to overhear the tale of my bird-charming flute, and as a result I spent three days pursuing Goldie round Regents Park, blasting away on this wretched instrument while a cameraman filmed the whole ludicrous operation. I did not of course succeed in charming Goldie back into his cage, and it was another ten days before he succumbed to the temptation of a succulent rabbit and landed within reach of his keepers. At least it should have taught me the lesson that it is unwise to return from royal tours and tell flippant tales about them. Alas, as must be apparent, and indeed as many luncheon clubs will confirm, I have been telling them ever since.

Chapter Nine

So far my overseas assignments had been 'diary jobs', predictable affairs which could be planned ahead, with a beginning, a middle and an end, but new developments had been taking place back home, giving far greater opportunities for the reporters. News Division moved from its homely surroundings in Egton House to spacious new offices in the Broadcasting House Extension. There Tom Maltby transformed himself from 'Reporting Organiser' into the far more imposing 'Head of Home Correspondents and Reporters', and set about creating an empire worthy of the title. More reporters were taken on, mostly 'hard news' men from the popular dailies. There were men like Peter Woon, former air correspondent of the *Express*, eventually to become Editor of Radio News, and Peter Woods, ex-crime man on the *Mirror* and former correspondent with the Suez landings, now leading a more sedate life as a newsreader. There was also a virtual unknown called Frederick Forsyth, who went to Biafra for the BBC, decided to join in, and re-emerged some years later with a book called *The Day of the Jackal*. Freddie said recently he did not fancy returning to radio because it involved getting up too early, and I know what he means. It just goes to show that the earliest bird does not always catch the fattest worm.

This new intake of seasoned Fleet Street men, most of them with overseas experience and used to working fast and sometimes ruthlessly against competition, coincided with more foreign assignments to back up our resident correspondents abroad. Reporters now became an international 'fire brigade', and television was using far more of our own material in preference to agency film. New titles were devised to give reporters greater responsibilities and more mobility in their specialised fields, and we found ourselves with a science correspondent, an economics correspondent, education and ecclesiastical correspondents and, to cover any gaps in all that, a home affairs correspondent. The reporters' offices no longer had the leisurely atmosphere of a club smoking-room. An Oxbridge accent was no longer as important as a good contacts book, a shrewd eye for a new angle, and a skin like a rhinoceros. The ladies in Facilities no longer had time to write out in their elegant longhand 'Please go in the first place to Margate Information Bureau – turn left outside the station'; now it was just a handful of travellers' cheques and an airline ticket, here's the phone number of our local man, and we'll tell you where you are staying after you get there.

Slightly bewildered, I found myself swept up in this dramatic new world of the permanently packed suitcase and the dash to the airport. On 11 November 1965, Ian Smith in Rhodesia made his unilateral declaration of independence and two hours later still gulping, I was on my way to Central Africa. It was my first major overseas assignment for Television News, and it looked like being a spectacular one. The situation in Rhodesia had been building up for a couple of years, ever since the break-up of the Central African Federation. Nyasaland had become an independent Malawi under Hastings Banda, Northern Rhodesia an independent Zambia under Kenneth Kaunda; only Southern Rhodesia was left, the white population still determined not to allow African rule. Talks with Harold Wilson failed to break the deadlock, and on 11 November Smith declared UDI, stating; 'We have struck a blow for the preservation of justice, civilisation and Christianity.' The cheers could be heard from Salisbury to Bulawayo, and white Rhodesians stood by to man the barricades.

With me on the plane was a television news camera team, fortunately far more experienced in these situations than I was: Tony Griggs, a meditative New Zealander and that rare bird among international newsmen, a teetotaller, and Bob Catlow, doyen of the sound recordists, rotund and imperturbable, whether it was on the lawns of Petworth House or looking for guerrillas along the Zambesi. They were a splendid couple to be with on one's first big foreign story.

We were heading for Lusaka, Zambia's capital, with the brief to cover the activities on the Zambian side of the border, to keep an eye on the border itself, and to make sure that we had some film in the camera when the fighting actually broke out. The point was that although Rhodesia was supposed to be under siege, in fact it was Zambia that was likely to suffer most if trouble started. Zambia is the world's third largest copper producer, after America and Russia, and its Copper Belt is the backbone of the economy, but the bulk of its output was exported at that time by rail through Rhodesia, on trains controlled by Rhodesians. Furthermore, all of Zambia's power supplies came from the Kariba hydro-electric plant on the border, with the control room on the Rhodesian side. Even the arrivals and departures at Lusaka Airport were handled by air traffic controllers in Salisbury, and it was typical of the interdependence between these former twin colonies that to reach Lusaka we had to fly via Salisbury. It was equally typical of air travel that we missed our connecting flight and had to spend a night in what, according to our brief, was the wrong side of the lines.

Salisbury, not surprisingly, was in a state of high excitement. There was no doubt about the backing for Smith and UDI but already, and even in the few hours we were there, we could detect a certain apprehension about what might happen next. It was not the fear of actual attack – nobody there expected British troops to be used, and the sabre-rattling by the African states was apparently not taken too seriously – but everyone appreciated what economic difficulties could lie ahead if sanctions were really effective.

In Lusaka the journalists were arriving hourly from all corners of the globe. Some of them I had men on the tours, but mostly I knew them only through their by-lines on the front pages – tough characters who roamed the trouble spots of the world, who could somehow always get a room in a hotel already full, and always get a drink when the last bar had shut. They virtually took over the Ridgeway Hotel, buttonholing Zambian officials in the foyer, queuing by the telephone switchboard, bribing the porter for the next taxi, carting off vast reserves of liquor to their rooms. Over it all, the chatter of typewriter keys mingled with the chirping of the cicadas as we set the scene for Central Africa to burst into flames.

In fact all that happened was that Kaunda's appeals for British support produced a token force of jet fighters, which flew into Lusaka Airport under the guidance of the air traffic controllers in Salisbury; I wish we could have recorded the exchanges between pilots and control tower! They parked around the perimeter, the Zambians admired them for a day or two, then they gradually merged into the scenery. Mr Arthur Bottomley flew out to give the President some verbal encouragement but very little else. In Addis Ababa the OAU threatened to break off diplomatic relations with Britain if the Rhodesian rebellion was not ended within twelve

85

days. After twelve days the rebellion, and Britain, still survived, and so did the Zambian economy. In the Ridgeway Hotel we ate our umpteenth chicken-in-a-basket, noted how the other correspondents were thinning out, and started thinking about home.

We made one foray across the Zambesi. The main road bridge was still open, if you had the right kind of passport and the right colour of skin, and apart from an extensive search of the camera equipment we had no trouble. The lumbering Pontiac we had hired now found itself for the first time on Rhodesian soil. Like Zambian soil, it was very, very dusty.

Here too it was becoming apparent that no sudden holocaust was about to burst around us. The Africans appeared uncommonly content with what seemed to a visiting European to be a depressing and humiliating existence. The townships looked like down-at-heel barracks, while those Africans who lived with European families had bleak little huts at the end of a garden, where in other circumstances you might expect to find a donkey or a goat. Yet the Europeans assured us that they were better off there than in their native surroundings and manifestly believed what they said. They were genuinely astonished that anyone could think the Africans capable of governing themselves. They treated them like lazy but not unlovable children, and they found it quite astonishing that some of the 'children' were trying to pretend they were grown up. It seemed to them completely right that those who displayed such precociousness, like Joshua Nkomo and Ndabaningi Sithole, should be made to stand in a corner – if necessary for several years.

These white Rhodesians were in the main sensible, hard-working, likeable people and, as they never stopped reminding us, they were our kith and kin. After all, they would tell us, they had lived there all their lives, we had been there for three days. I met Round Tablers in Salisbury and Bulawayo who were just as genial and good-hearted as Tablers at home, who worked just as hard for charity, who pursued the same aims and objects as we did, and who had the same motto: 'Adopt, Adapt, Improve'. This, they reckoned, was precisely what they were doing for the five and a half million Africans in Rhodesia. Since there are twenty-three Africans to every European that argument can hardly be entirely specious, or they would have been wiped out within weeks, but it is not an argument they can maintain indefinitely, and even then I think they knew it.

86

When we left Rhodesia and re-crossed the Zambesi, Central Africa had still not burst into flames, and no amount of speculation could suggest that it would. In spite of the histrionics and the threats and the forebodings, any likelihood of trouble was diminishing every day. Around the lily pond at the Ridgeway the last of the correspondents were packing their bags. Two days before Christmas came the cable to pack ours.

The Rhodesia-Zambia situation simmered on through the winter. A frigate patrolled outside Beira as tangible evidence of the world's disapproval, and angry noises could be regularly heard from the UN and Westminster and Addis Ababa. Meanwhile I was back on the home circuit, touring the North on George Brown's election tour (during which, contrary to popular belief, he drank only tomato juice), then reporting from Liberal Headquarters on election night (there was not of course much to report), then over to Dublin for a nostalgic feature on the fiftieth anniversary of the Easter Rising. How peaceful that visit was, compared with later ones in the north. I even revisited the paths of royalty with a State Visit to Brussels, and watched some very fancy flag-waving in the Grande Place. It all seemed a long way from the tense days in Zambia, yet in May I was back on the Zambesi again.

The row this time was over the railway. The dire predictions made back in November, that if Rhodesia closed the railway then the Copper Belt would come to a standstill, now looked like coming true. It had started over the transfer of money from Zambia to Rhodesia: Rhodesia demanded payment in advance for copper shipments, Zambia refused on the grounds that they could not go on condoning illegality indefinitely. Rhodesia threatened to hold up the copper shipments, Zambia stopped railway imports. It looked like the crunch at last.

To me it looked almost like home. There was the lily pond, there were the chickens in the same old baskets, there even was the old Pontiac, nose already pointed towards the Zambesi. This time the camera crew was Ted Studd, a heavily moustached extrovert who had seen it all and enjoyed a large proportion of it, and his quieter sidekick, Gerry Goad. Off we went, sending back speculation pieces: 'This is the railhead in the Copper Belt, and that may be the last load of copper to get out of the country.' South to Lusaka, to film the same train as it trundled through. 'This is Lusaka Station, and that may be the last load of copper

. . .' South again to the railway bridge across the Zambesi, alongside the Victoria Falls. 'This is the Zambesi, and that may be the last load . . .' No wonder back at Alexandra Palace the film editors came to greet our despatches with the cry, 'Here's another load of old copper!'

It was not until 8 June, after a great deal of copper had rolled over the bridges, that the mining companies suspended shipments through Rhodesia, not because the Rhodesians had finally refused to accept it, but because they suspected it was all being held up in the railway yards at Wankie. (I never achieved an ambition to round off a despatch with 'John Timpson, BBC, Wankie'!) The Zambians started developing their alternative routes – the antique Benguela railway through the Congo, and the appalling road through Tanzania to Dar-es-Salaam. Meanwhile the British started an oil lift into Zambia to replace the railway supplies, and a vague sort of petrol rationing was introduced which could have grounded our thirsty old Pontiac if it had been strictly enforced.

Again it became apparent that the expected confrontation was not going to happen. Zambia was going to pull through; Rhodesia had never looked as though it would not. We interviewed President Kaunda, surely the most charming and least excitable of African leaders, and found that he too foresaw no imminent conflagration. So again we pulled out of Central Africa after reporting a story which had never actually happened. We had not heard a shot fired, nor seen a hand raised in anger. Our only injury was a nastily scalded chest which Ted Studd had suffered when he rashly removed the radiator cap after the Pontiac had boiled over on one of our copper chases. As for me, I never wanted to see a chicken in a basket again.

Again I returned to the home rota, which brought me my first encounter with the redoubtable Reverend Ian Paisley, an occasion which I believe is still recalled with relish by BBC men in Belfast. As Dr Paisley emerged from a spell in Belfast Jail it was my task to approach him for his first thoughts on his incarceration. I introduced myself as a representative of the BBC.

'Which BBC?' demanded Dr Paisley, meaning, as I discovered later, was I a local man or from London.

Quite baffled by this at the time, I could only register hurt surprise. 'Sir,' I said with as much dignity as I could muster, 'there is only one BBC.' There was some discreet applause from the camera crew, and in Belfast my reputation as a wag was made.

It was Dr Paisley, however, who laughed last. At an open air meeting he addressed some two thousand of his supporters, and I was perched on a car roof in the midst of them. It was a typical display of Paisleyan pyrotechnics, and the crowd was with him to a man. At the climax of his speech, with his audience roaring their support, the good cleric cried out dramatically: 'Whose fault is it? It is the fault of the BBC!' – and pointed directly at me. Two thousand enraged Ulstermen turned towards me, and suddenly I longed for the peace and quiet of a little guerrilla warfare along the Zambesi. As it happened he turned his sights on some other target, and when I talked to him later he was affability itself, but that was the last time in Northern Ireland that I ever stood on a car roof to get a better view.

As it turned out, this was only an interlude before I was involved in the next act in the Rhodesia negotiations. On my return to London I was sent on a routine assignment to Heathrow, to describe Mr Wilson's departure for the meeting with Mr Smith on HMS *Tiger*, berthed in Gibraltar Docks. I was to provide the standard commentary for the cameras: 'There he goes now for one of the most dramatic encounters in modern political history' – then help pack up the camera gear and go home for tea. But as we waited for the plane to leave, a message came from the office we must go to Gibraltar too.

This time I had no packed suitcase in the boot. Actually I never believed this sort of thing ever really happened, and after keeping a spare shirt in the boot for a while and finding it impregnated with petrol fumes and mildew, I had never bothered about it since. Even more unforgivable, I had no passport with me either. It was sheer luck I even had my tape-recorder. Such is the remarkable world-wide prestige of the BBC everywhere except among its own viewers and listeners at home, I was able to get out to Gibraltar and home again on nothing more substantial than my BBC pass. Admittedly those were pre-terrorist days, and I doubt it could be done now, but even then I was quite impressed.

With me went Bert Foote and Tony Macpherson, a genial and gentlemanly camera team who were as surprised as I was by this turn of events. Together we caught a plane a few minutes after the Prime Minister's, and thanks to some splendid liaison work by our local man in Gibraltar we actually got to the docks ahead of Mr Wilson and filmed him driving through the gates. It was just as well, because throughout his negotiations with Mr Smith we never caught sight of him again. This did not of course prevent us sending back our regular speculative reports, in which I was rapidly becoming an expert. 'These are the dock gates, beyond which lies HMS *Tiger*, where the fate of Rhodesia is being decided. Or: 'This is Gibraltar beach, and across that bay lies HMS *Tiger* . . .' Or: 'This is Gibraltar's main street, as busy as ever, while a quarter of a mile away . . .' Finally a rather traumatic one: 'This is the Rock, home of the Barbary apes, while far beneath me . . .' It was traumatic because while I was addressing the camera one adventurous ape seized me by the upper leg and made a determined effort to undo my trousers. I gather the close-ups of my expression during this performance were a tremendous draw, back in the editing rooms.

We did eventually film in HMS *Tiger*, and I was actually able to say at last 'This is HMS *Tiger* . . .' Alas, it was only after the meetings were over and the protagonists had departed. Mr Wilson went back to London, convinced that a settlement was assured, while Mr Smith went back to Salisbury to get the approval of his Cabinet. That was on the Sunday morning. By Monday night the Rhodesian Cabinet had turned down the proposals and Smith was announcing 'The fight will go on', as indeed it did throughout the next decade. Meanwhile Bert, Tony and I packed our new toothbrushes and took ourselves off to the airport, crumpled and passport-less. We talked our way through passport control at Heathrow and, three days late, went home for tea.

Chapter Ten

The Rhodesian stories ended bloodlessly, but I was not always to be so fortunate – or, in journalistic terms, so unfortunate. Now I was a fully fledged member of the 'fire brigade' and a series of overseas assignments came my way which were at best rather uncomfortable and at worst downright terrifying. The first actually occurred en route to my second tour of duty in Zambia. We had reached Nairobi when the news came from neighbouring Uganda that a state of emergency had been declared, and a showdown was taking place between Milton Obote and the Kabaka of Buganda, 'King Freddie'. Obote, who had been prime minister since independence three years before, had just responded to charges of corruption by taking over all the powers of government himself, putting five ministers in detention, suspending the constitution and declaring himself president, the office previously held by the Kabaka. King Freddie and his followers protested vigorously, and Obote laid siege to his palace.

It was at this stage that we were diverted to Kampala, to find a town under martial law with security forces patrolling the streets, controlling the approaches and completely encircling the hill on which the Kabaka's palace stood. We attempted to film it from neighbouring high ground but were chased away by troops. However, Ted Studd did get some useful film of all the military activity, I provided the standard helping of speculation, and we took it to Entebbe Airport for shipment home.

On the way back to Kampala we ran into trouble. The road was blocked by troops and every car was being stopped and searched. Any African drivers and passengers were being hauled out, shoved into the ditch, and in some cases clouted with rifle butts. It was my first sight of how an armed African is inclined to treat an unarmed one, and very unsavoury it was. Fortunately in those pre-Amin days the British were still treated warily, and when it came to our turn they became reasonably civil, until they found the camera gear in the boot. This they did not take kindly to at all. A great hullabaloo arose, the NCO in charge began a tirade about imperialist spies, and his men ostentatiously released their safety catches. They stood in line across the road with their rifles held diagonally across their chests, and the wild thought struck me that if we had to make a dash for it, it would only need one sharp nudge on the man at the end of the row for the whole lot to wipe themselves out.

Fortunately it did not come to this, but we were instructed to drive into Kampala with a sergeant sitting beside me in the back seat, and report to the police station. The sergeant's rifle also appeared to be cocked, and I had never known Ted drive with such caution round the potholes or pull up so gently at the intersections. To our profound relief a British officer received us at the police station, checked our BBC passes and sent us back to our hotel. They say no foreign correspondent's training is complete until he has been arrested, and you get extra marks for being actually imprisoned or expelled, but that made the experience no pleasanter at the time.

That same day Obote's troops took the palace, King Freddie fled into exile, and unreluctantly we moved on to what seemed the bigger story in Zambia. Five years later Obote himself was overthrown by Idi Amin and likewise went into exile, but the sad King Freddie only returned to his country in a coffin, after his death in London, to be given a state burial and to close the chapter which we had seen open so abruptly.

A year later I was under arrest again, in another police station, after another coup d'etat. In May 1967 the Colonels took over in Greece, and I was despatched to Athens with a camera crew. Within an hour of arrival we were filming tanks in the streets; within two hours of arrival we were under arrest, the film was confiscated, and we were told very firmly that the only military material we could photograph was the ceremonial guard in their frills and pompoms. Encouraged by this official guidance, our cameraman Peter Matthews did just that – and by a happy chance frequently found himself including tanks and armed patrols in the background.

Having now got the pictures we had wanted in the first place, we found the Customs were not accepting any film for shipment, certainly not forbidden film of Army activity. We therefore had to rely on the goodwill of returning British passengers to smuggle the film out for us, and this they did on the whole most willingly; I suppose there is a little of James Bond in us all. We could hardly approach them in the main concourse of the air terminal, under the eyes of the security men, so all our importuning was done in the only place that offered sufficient privacy, the men's lavatory. The procedure could well have got us arrested again on a totally different charge, but we suffered nothing worse than an over-friendly nudge from the attendant.

After some days it became apparent that no counter-coup was likely, and the colonels were firmly in charge. It was time to move on, in my case to Sicily to film a feature about the Mafia with Bernard Hesketh, as a number of leading 'godfathers' had just been rounded up. It no doubt seemed a good idea back at Alexandra Palace, but the Mafiosi do not go about wearing badges, nor do they always carry black violin cases, and if we did meet any of them I never knew it. But Bernard took some splendid pictures of the mean back-alleys in Palermo and the bleak little villages in the hills, and I did a vague commentary hinting that these might be Mafia strongholds – as indeed they might for all I knew – and somehow we conjured up a comprehensive survey of the Sicilian Mafia in a three-and-a-half-minute film.

From sombre Sicily we crossed to Malta en fête. It was another State Visit, and we spent a pleasant week filming the handshakes and the bouquets, but as we reached the final stages I was restless for home. On the last night we celebrated into the early hours, then returned to the hotel to pick up our bags for the breakfasttime flight to London. A cable awaited us: 'Change of plan fly Cyprus soonest to cover new crisis.'

Bernard was delighted; he was eager for a change from the royal circuit, and Gerry Goad, his sound recordist, felt the same. But back home we had recently moved into a rather pleasant house in Chorleywood; a bedroom needed decorating, there was work to do in the garden, the woods we backed on to had yet to be explored. The presents for Pat and the boys were in my suitcase, I could already savour that first pint in my own armchair. I think Bernard and Gerry were quite startled when I threw a small portable radio, very hard indeed, against the bedroom wall.

It was not the proper reaction of a dedicated journalist, and this was the moment when I knew that a lifelong role as a globetrotting, troubleshooting reporter was not really for me. This was not the time to argue, though. The London flight left without us, and we headed eastwards to Nicosia, to that famous haunt of international newsmen in time of crisis, the Ledra Palace Hotel. It was right on the United Nations 'Green Line' separating the Greek-Cypriot and Turkish-Cypriot quarters, with a UN checkpoint under my window and UN troops patrolling the corridors. 'An ideal situation,' said our Foreign Desk. 'If they start shooting, you'll be the first to know.' Fortunately at that time they didn't. We spent much of our time pacing the beach at Kyrenia, waiting for the Turkish Navy to land, but it was another seven years before the Turks invaded; it was decided, to my relief, that we could not wait that long.

There were to be two more overseas assignments before I moved into the studio: to Austria with the Queen, a predictably peaceful affair where my most daring exploit was to hire a carriage for a pictorial horse-drawn tour of Vienna, later to startle the accounts department with my Holmes-like expenses, 'To hire of fiacre. . .'; and then to the Lebanon with Bernard, which was not peaceful at all.

It was October 1969, and not for the first time nor the last, the Palestinian guerrillas in their refugee camps around Beirut were showing signs of impatience and unrest. There was also friction between the Christian and Muslim Lebanese, which was to lead to the virtual civil war of 1975, but at that time it was the Palestine Liberation Organisation causing the trouble and there were strong fears that the Syrians would move into Lebanon to support them. The Syrian border was closed, and the next time it opened, so the theory went, the hordes of the Syrians would be seen in the land.

As soon as we arrived at the airport a message awaited me demanding an immediate filmed despatch. This comprehensive summary of the situation, recorded some ten minutes after I had first set foot on Lebanese soil, apparently made quite an impact. 'Thanks speedy start,' said a cable that night from Newscasts, the telegraphic title of the BBC. 'First report made very worthwhile one forty-one Newsroom and National.' That meant one minute forty-one seconds on both BBC1 and BBC2, equivalent to a front page spread in the *Telegraph* and the *Guardian*, and from then on the pace never slackened.

This was entirely due to the enthusiasm of Bernard Hesketh and his sound recordist, Bill Nicol. There was street fighting going on in Beirut and Tripoli, and I would have much preferred to report it from my hotel window, a ploy not unknown among

'Have Press Passes, will travel' – to Cyprus (both Greek and Turkish), Tunisia, Woolwich. The Russian visa, to report on Princess Anne riding in Kiev, was never actually used as the Soviet broadcasting authorities found they could not provide facilities.

foreign correspondents. But Bernard is incorrigible on such occasions, and once his eye is behind a viewfinder the world around him becomes just a picture in a frame. I can understand how cameramen can get so detached from what they are filming that they still keep pressing the button until, as actually happened in one case, a real bullet can emerge from that picture and kill them, but I possessed no such ring of confidence, and I was mostly petrified.

In Tripoli, Bernard persuaded me to do a piece to camera outside the old castle in the town centre at a time when it was being sniped at from surrounding streets. I am told that my look of agonised apprehension conveyed the gravity of the situation far better than any words I may have spoken. Later, on a road beside the Syrian border, we ran into the sort of story which Bernard might have arranged himself: we heard a burst of firing, a mortar shell landed in a field beside us, and it became apparent that we had wandered into an ambush. I have never got out of a car and underneath it quite so fast. Most of my reporting colleagues have been in far worse spots than this, whether in Northern Ireland or Vietnam or Angola. Get them together over a few beers and they will tell you tales which make that afternoon by the Syrian border seem like an old folks' mystery outing. But this was the first time poeple had actually shot at me on purpose, and I found it extremely disconcerting. Not so Bernard, of course. He was crawling cheerfully around with his camera, trying to spot our attackers, filming the explosions, and urging me to perform, of all things, a stand-up piece to camera.

I stammered a few words into Bill Nicol's microphone from somewhere beneath the back axle, Bernard's film as always was immaculate, and eventually they knitted the whole thing together back home and made quite an effective little drama out of it. Thanks to Bernard's utter disregard for keeping out of trouble, and my own inability to say no, we managed to get a fair amount of action coverage, and the 'herograms' kept coming in. 'Like predecessor, your Rachaiya report highly praised'; 'Continuing success Masna report'; and so on. On the night before we were due to return home there appeared a rather different cable: 'Proceed Amman immediately for interview Hussein and Habash.' It turned out to be just Bernard having his little joke and hoping I would smash another radio, as indeed I nearly did, but I did not need this reminder of my reaction that early morning in Valetta, two years before. My mind was already made up.

By all accounts our Lebanon assignment was a success. The report of the senior foreign duty editor read: 'One difficult assignment with outstandingly successful results was John Timpson's to the Lebanon, with the Hesketh/Nicol camera team. They provided a series of dramatic, on-the-spot reports on the fighting between Government and guerrilla forces.' A year or two earlier such a commendation might have tempted me to stay on the road, to try to become another René Cutforth or James Cameron. Now it merely seemed a good note on which to 'come inside'.

There is much to be said for being a member of the 'fire brigade', and I count myself lucky to have had the experience. It was always unpredictable, often dramatic, occasionally momentous. It took me to places and people I would never otherwise have encountered, and there were times when I was privileged to see history in the making. But it can also be exasperating, unrewarding and tedious in the extreme. For every moment of exhilarating excitement there are hours of boredom in an airport lounge or a hotel bedroom or even a prison cell. There is indeed glamour and glory, but there is also disruption and discomfort and sometimes distaste. It is a life for which you need to be young, fit and energetic, preferably with no family ties or social commitments, inspired either by dedication or by a certain degree of dementia. I no longer qualified under any of these headings. I was into my forties, I had a growing family which I liked to be with, and Pat had borne the brunt of this unbalanced existence long enough. They let me hang up my fireman's helmet in favour of more weighty, less volatile equipment, as I left the 'brigade' to become a full-time 'anchorman' instead.

Chapter Eleven

New techniques in the presentation of Television News had been experimented with ever since the BBC's second channel opened in 1964. In fact the first experiment went out on the air rather earlier than anyone had foreseen, because on the opening night of the new channel, after a tremendous publicity build-up, a power failure blacked out the Television Centre just before transmission and the only studio still able to function was the news studio at Alexandra Palace. Gerry Priestland, one of the early reporter-presenters on BBC2, found himself ad-libbing to the nation at one of the most historic moments in the BBC's existence.

For some time after that we continued rather to make up news programmes as we went along, but the general pattern was a five-minute bulletin in the early evening and an extended twenty-minute news magazine much later on. For the first time reporters were able to present their own stories in the studio, and the bulletins themselves were presented by other reporters like Gerry Priestland, Peter Woon, and in due course myself. We were all trained journalists and as far as possible we wrote our scripts ourselves. This was real 'newcasting' as opposed to 'newsreading' on BBC1, in the sense that we had a hand in casting the shape and content of the bulletin instead of merely reading the material which other people had provided. We could cope with live interviews in the studio, and in emergencies could ad-lib news stories from the bare bones of agency tape. We probably lacked the polish and the faultless enunciation of our BBC1 colleagues, but we were achieving on television the same kind of authoritative and personalised news presentation that 'The World At One' was later to achieve on radio.

While the main effort was going into the late bulletin, I was involved in a fascinating experiment with the earlier five-minute summary. It was decided that we should pack into that summary as many news items as would normally be carried in a radio summary, the catch being of course that we not only had to condense each story into fifteen seconds, we had to do it with pictures too. This involved some of the most adroit editing and the crispest scripting in the news business. For a start you avoided words like 'crispest scripting' – by the time you had wrapped your tongue around that, they were two stories ahead of you with the film. We prided ourselves on the presenter appearing in vision for only a few seconds throughout the five minutes, and we engaged in all manner of pictorial juggling to keep him off the screen. It was this bulletin, I suspect, which inspired David Frost's famous reference to the Lord (picture of a lord) Privy (picture of a privy) Seal (picture of a seal). It was also a technical miracle and great fun, but I doubt if a viewer absorbed more than one story in six, and indeed if he sneezed he probably missed the other five altogether. Eventually we slowed down to a gallop, and in later years the wheel turned full circle and the five minutes became a straight radio-style summary with no illustrations at all, the ultimate in talking-head television and enough to make viewers demand their money back.

Meanwhile the late-night programme was gaining in experience and efficiency and at the beginning of 1968 'Newsroom' was given the recognition it deserved when it was extended to a full half-hour and moved to the peak time of 7.30. Already the programme had pioneered the idea of dual presentation of the news, an idea subsequently adopted by the other two channels; now it became the first thirty-minute news bulletin without any time lost on commercials, and a few weeks later it was to be the first news programme to go into colour.

The switchover to colour was in one sense a dramatic step forward, in another sense just as dramatic a step backward. For the first time viewers could see what was going on in the world realistically, instead of in shades of black and white; on the other hand, the technical problems set back the news-gathering operation at Alexandra Palace by a good ten years: colour film required much longer and more complex processes for developing; thousands of colour slides had to be acquired to replace the old monochrome prints; graphics (the maps and diagrams used to illustrate news stories) had to be either put through a synthesiser, which turned black and white into two colours, or drawn afresh; and biggest drawback of all, none of the regions had facilities for transmitting colour videotape, so that instead of being 'piped down the line' in a matter of seconds from other parts of the country, the colour film itself had to be flown to

London. A light plane was constantly on call to bring the film to Leavesden Airport, near Watford, then a despatch rider brought it the final fifteen miles to Alexandra Palace. It was an operation which could waste hours of valuable time.

While the production team and the technical staff were grappling with these problems, quite different hazards were arising for those of us who were actually appearing in colour for the first time. We ran into trouble first over shirts. We were advised that in studio conditions it was not permissible to wear a white shirt; it would reflect the lights and dazzle the cameramen, and the picture would go fuzzy round the edges. On the other hand, shirts in a certain shade of blue were also banned, because of a device called colour separation overlay, or cso. As I understand it, cso involves a camera which is designed not to record anything which is in this particular shade of blue; it just leaves a hole instead. By putting an area of blue behind the presenter, directing another camera onto a different picture and mixing the two shots, you can make that second picture appear behind the presenter. That is how you can watch him reading the news while behind him appear all those pictures. but if the presenter himself looks round, all he can see is the blue square. The snag with cso is that if the presenter wears a blue shirt, or a blue tie, or even has blue bags under his eyes, then that other picture will not only appear behind him, it will also appear on his shirt, or on his tie, or under his eyes. It is possible to achieve the weird effect of a newscaster with tanks trundling across his stomach or Mr Wilson peering out of his tie.

There was also 'strobing', brought about by a check shirt or jacket. If the colours were too close together they would shimmer in a most distracting fashion. One only needed a blue tie to absorb the overlay, a white shirt to dazzle the cameras, and a check jacket to start the strobing, and the general effect was rather like the Trafalgar Square Christmas tree. In view of all this, we thought it not unreasonable to suggest that the bbc might come up with a shirt or two for us. We wrote to our masters, pointing out that as loyal servants of the Corporation we had always made a point of wearing white shirts to the office, and now we were expected to transform our entire wardrobe. All we received in reply was a memo saying the problem was appreciated, and thank you for mentioning it, and please 'phase out' your white shirts. Actually they did introduce a modest dress allowance, but we must have presented a strange sight during the next few weeks, chaps creosoting their fences and cleaning out their oil sumps and scrubbing out their garages, all wearing immaculate white shirts – phasing them out.

It was the problem of make-up, however, which taxed us most. In the old days of black and white television (or monochrome, as it was officially called, perhaps to avoid offending anybody), we merely applied a little powder to the forehead to reduce the shine. But in front of a colour camera, if you have just powdered yourself it quite often looks as if you have just powdered yourself, and we found that people were getting a totally wrong impression of life in the BBC. We were therefore each inspected by three ladies from the make-up department, who offered us advice on how to enhance our appearance without taking things too far. When it came to my turn, however, it became apparent that even the BBC make-up department has its limitations. They studied me with obvious distaste, then disappeared, shaking their heads. Eventually, though, they returned in triumph. My difficulty, they explained, was an oversaturated face. This seemed an offensive phrase, but it was merely make-up department jargon to describe my permanent rosy flush, a legacy perhaps from those bracing Norfolk winters or, more likely, from all that bracing Norfolk ale. I gathered that they had been grappling with this problem in the laboratory and had now come up with this magical make-up for unfortunate people like me. The official name for it was Toasted Beige, and it turned out to be a light mud-coloured mixture, applied with a small sponge.

They showed me how to douse my oversaturated cheeks with a layer of Toasted Beige, and added some further advice: 'Don't put it just on your face.'

'Where else,' I asked, 'do you have in mind?'

It turned out to be the ears. Some of the studio lights are behind the presenter and they shine forwards through the ears, making him look rather like a taxi with indicators on the roof turning left and right simultaneously. A spongeful of Toasted Beige in each ear was the answer, and another spongeful applied to the backs of the hands prevented the fingers from looking like uncooked sausages. In fact we almost had to bath in the stuff, but even then it was not entirely successful because it gradually started to fade in the heat from the lights. As the programme progressed we would find the cheeks oversaturating again, and the ears lighting up, and the bulletin would take on almost a party atmosphere.

To counter this phenomenon a make-up girl would regularly appear in the studio about halfway through the programme, wait until a film was running so that viewers could not see what was happening, and attack the presenters with spongefuls of Toasted Beige. It was my constant hope that the girl would be too slow and the film too quick, and that the nation would get a glimpse of its favourite newscasters being sponged down like a secondhand car. It never actually happened, but whenever I watch a particularly doom-laden bulletin I still cheer myself up just visualising the possibilities.

The new improved 'Newsroom' with the added colour ingredient was largely the responsibility of Peter Woon, who had made the rare move from a reporter's desk to an editor's chair. Its two regular presenters were also from the reporters' room, Peter Woods and myself. Indeed, as Peter Woon wrote at the time in *Radio Times*, it was really a reporters' programme. Our extra time made it possible to use longer, better planned, in-depth reports instead of the brief snatches on BBC1. 'Among journalists generally,' wrote Peter, 'there are often arguments about whether broadcasting is in competition with the newspapers. We have no doubts about it – we are.'

Even at the earlier, more popular hour, viewers were still thin on the ground. On two evenings a week, for instance, we clashed with 'Coronation Street'; there went umpteen million viewers for a start. I often felt that the only major difference between 'News at Ten' and 'Newsroom' was that they had twelve million viewers and we had our wives and mums. Among journalists, though, there was no doubt about the value of our experiment. The late Bill Hardcastle, to become famous for his similar pioneering work in radio, praised the separate style we had developed on BBC2 and our use of journalists instead of newsreaders. 'The idea,' he wrote, 'is obviously to project an added element of authority and involvement, though whether this gets across to the average viewer is difficult for someone like myself to judge.' I rather doubt that it did. They may have noticed that what Bill went on to call my 'wry, matter-of-fact style' (or 'wry and mocking' according to Bernard Hollowood, or 'urgent but not foaming' if you read Peter Black) was rather different from the deadpan approach of our announcer colleagues on BBC1. They may have detected a certain levity in some of the scripts which the sub-editors would not have permitted themselves on the senior channel. But the early ambitions of Peter Woon to make this a real 'reporter's programme', with members of the 'fire brigade' dashing into the studio fresh from the story, telephones ringing, carrier pigeons landing on the desk, an all-action, see-it-as-it-happens spectacular never really materialised.

There was only one occasion when 'Newsroom' really came into its own. It was during the Czechoslovakian crisis of August 1968. The brief period of freedom was over, Russian tanks were moving into Prague, and all official communications had been cut, but a handful of heroic cameramen and technicians were still filming in the city and smuggling the film out of the country. It so happened that the pictures reached Alexandra Palace while 'Newsroom' was on the air. With me in the studio was Hugh Lunghi, head of the BBC's Czech Service. Throughout the programme we had film coming into the building and being transmitted within minutes of its arrival, unseen by us beforehand, unedited, unscripted. As it went out, Hugh provided an impromptu commentary, translating the slogans on the banners, explaining where events were taking place, identifying the personalities involved. It was an astonishing feat: from this uncut film, often blurred or shaky as the cameraman took cover, Hugh was able to tell the story of the occupation of Prague, almost street by street. Even when one film came up in reverse, and vehicles appeared bearing Russian slogans written backwards, Hugh still succeeded in translating them.

We had two or three evenings like this, with the whole country tuned in to us. Nancy Banks-Smith, not always the kindest of critics, called it a 'minute-by-minute cliffhanger. On such a night as this,' she wrote, 'BBC television can pull out stops that ITV just have not got on the keyboard.' Peter Black wrote that 'viewers were given as direct and stirring a sense of participation in what was happening as is possible for a television picture to do . . . See-it-now brought to Television News an impact that no other medium can match.'

Hugh Lunghi was the real star, but some of the glory was reflected and after three years of oblivion it was gratifying to read of my 'well trained understanding of the blend of intimacy and urgency that newsreading needs', of how I 'kept firm control of what was going on, often a confused and rushed sequence of false starts and delays, without being caught with egg on the face'. More practical recognition came from within the BBC: David Attenborough, then Controller of BBC2, wrote that we had shown the full potential of 'Newsroom' and substantially enlarged not only the stature of the programme but my own personal reputation as well. His letter was accompanied by a hundred-pound bonus. To quote Peter Black once more, that evil wind did 'Newsroom' a good turn. Mercifully for the world, but unfortunately for programmes like 'Newsroom', such evil winds do not occur that often and in the year or two that followed I do not recall 'Newsroom's' full potential ever being demonstrated again.

The programme gradually developed along more orthodox lines to become more and more like a half-hour version of the BBC1 bulletin, sometimes padded out rather desperately with what one critic referred to as films about the decline of the hake-fishing industry in Carmarthenshire. Towards the end of 1969 two events occurred which in my view ended any hope of 'Newsroom' achieving its original objectives. Peter Woon moved to Broadcasting House to become Editor, Radio News, and the entire Television News operation moved from Alexandra Palace to the Spur, the new extension at the Television Centre. The team was much the same but the captain had left and the team spirit was lost in the greater world of the Centre. The new facilities were magnificent, but we were no longer a separate entity, an independent unit with its own character, its own eccentricities and its own rather swashbuckling approach to BBC administration. In those early days at any rate, it seemed to some of us that we were trying to report life in the real world outside while surrounded by showbiz make-believe.

Naturally there were compensations. The life of a 'Newsroom' presenter at the Centre was gentlemanly in the extreme: arrive after lunch, pen a few early stories, rehearse and present the programme, take a leisurely dinner, help to rewrite the main stories for the late-evening summary (now transferred from its earlier time), and with any luck get home by midnight. Then take one or two days off to recover. We had personal dressing rooms, a few fans, a little glory occasionally when we were recognised in the street. It was comfortable, congenial, and getting more and more routine.

I knew I wanted a change, but to what? The big current affairs

Paterfamilias with Pat, Jeremy and Nicholas.

programmes on television already had more anchormen than they knew what to do with. I might have rejoined the 'fire brigade', but I had already decided I had been on the road long enough. The only other possibility at the Television Centre was to apply for a desk job in the newsroom, the normal route to any sort of editorial or administrative ladder, but unless I became an Attenborough or a Humphrey Burton this would mean an end to actually performing, and I still relished the roar of the producer, the smell of the Toasted Beige.

There was only one place in the BBC for a presenter who wanted to combine news experience with a little light relief, where there was the excitement of reporting the major news stories and the freedom to chuckle at the silly ones, only one job which offered a reasonably settled working pattern while being flexible enough to handle the unexpected, and where studio work was occasionally leavened by excursions elsewhere. It was a live programme, informative yet informal, fast but not furious, 'hard-newsy' but still human. It was a radio programme with a television-size audience, an old favourite with a new future, and it was still called 'Today'. In January 1970 I called on the newly appointed editor of a newly created group called Morning Current Affairs Programmes (Radio).

Marshall Stewart was a comparative newcomer to be given such a responsibility. He had arrived at Broadcasting House, in the newsroom, after I had moved almost permanently to Alexandra Palace and our paths had not crossed before. He had made a spectacular name for himself in the South-East Region News, enlivening it with ambitious 'hook-ups' round the region, motoring 'flashes', outside broadcasts from a boat in mid-Channel or a helicopter in mid-flight – familiar techniques for the big occasion but unheard of in the modest, 'ship-spotters club' world of regional broadcasting. In the brave new era of broadcasting in the seventies, with its high-speed, all-action, catch-'em-by-the-ears-and-shake-'em radio news, Marshall was a rising star. As he explained to me his plans for 'Today', the new ideas he wanted to introduce, the new image he wanted it to achieve, it was impossible not to be impressed. His picture of how he wanted the programme presented coincided entirely with mine, and although we were to differ over the years on some of the features he introduced, the basic aims on which we agreed at that meeting for the atmosphere and character of the programme never changed.

I had a month's trial run. It seemed to work. On April the First, a not insignificant date, I bade farewell to Television News and indeed to News Division itself and was attached to Morning Current Affairs Programmes (Radio) as joint presenter with Jack de Manio on 'Today'.

Chapter Twelve

Jack had presented 'Today' for the previous twelve years. Indeed, to most of its five million listeners he *was* the 'Today' programme. Now he not only had a co-presenter foisted on him, but the whole character of the programme was being changed as well. He was being caught up in the new current affairs world of radio, what they were calling the Sound of the Seventies. One could have forgiven him if he had shown a little coolness towards the newcomer who must have epitomised the new order, but he did nothing of the sort. Instead he showed a tolerance and a kindliness throughout our twelve months together which helped to create a most congenial relationship, and I hope a flavour of it came through in the programme. There were many mornings when one or other of us felt like death, whether from a late night or an early cold, yet I do not recall us exchanging a single sour word.

It was not only 'Today' that was changing but the whole face of broadcasting, particularly on Radio 4, and particularly in news and current affairs. Radio bulletins were already being transformed by Peter Woon into a sound version of the 'Newsroom' programme he had created on television; true, the professional newsreader was still there, but reporters were voicing their own items, 'actuality' was being used increasingly, 'live' inserts were being encouraged. To the existing 'The World At One', now well established, there were added other personalised programmes throughout the day dealing in different aspects of the news: the 'PM' programme in the afternoon, 'Newsdesk' in the early evening, 'The World Tonight' replacing the 'Ten O'Clock' programme.

This left only one notable gap in Radio 4's current affairs coverage, in the period which offered more listeners than at any other hour of the day. It was not enough, they decided, for 'Today' to handle only the feature-page material, as it had mainly done for so long. Now it must include the front page, the sports page, the business pages and the international pages as well. This was why a journalist was made co-presenter, to 'harden' the programme. At the same time the sports department was handed a five-minute spot in each half of the programme and a third team member, Douglas Cameron, was brought in to handle the public service information about the roads and the trains and the weather. Jack was to handle mainly the lighter material, the traditional 'Today' items.

As it turned out the division of labour between Jack and myself was never as precise as that. Jack frequently handled news interviews, and to my relief I was permitted to handle the lighter items too. It became a team exercise, and because of its special problems no other programme requires teamwork quite so much. The hours in themselves were problem enough – the most affable of relationships can come under strain at seven in the morning – but there were also the hazards that any 'live' programme faces, where the unpredictable can always happen, a tape can snap, a connection can break or a guest can fail to appear. There were also less obvious booby-traps in the path of the unwary presenter, which to this day can implant egg all over the face.

These booby-traps are called regional opt-outs, which most listeners are probably aware of only when we fail to negotiate them; they are the moments when some part of the country with its own regional programme either leaves us or rejoins us, and to avoid unpleasant overlaps or embarrassing silences the timing has to be accurate to the second. At that period life on 'Today' was just one damn' opt-out after another: some regions would join us for the sports news at 7.25, others would leave us at 7.35 during the review of the papers, most of them returned at 7.45 for 'Thought for the Day', then left us again at 7.50 for their own regional news, came back again at 7.55 for the weather forecast, and so on. The programme progressed in a series of hiccups. Whatever was happening at those particular moments had to stop so that we could give a time-check and the engineers could change their lines.

This of course gave added significance to those time-checks for which Jack was so famous. His mistakes were not, as some cynics suggested, an intentional gimmick, he really did have difficulty telling the time. But it meant that if he was five minutes out, it not only got two or three million people out of bed in a devil of a hurry, it also caused considerable confusion in BBC control rooms all over the country. With the advent of local radio and some areas like Scotland and Northern Ireland now transmitting their own breakfast programmes (still using a lot of 'Today' material), the number of these opt-outs has mercifully diminished, but it is still possible to cause a fair old foul-up.

Ideally the programme was so constructed that items ended at the right moments, and the producer's task involved some lively mathematical gymnastics to bring this about, but with live interviews and variable reading speeds and always the likelihood of Jack holding up the proceedings with some unexpected observation on the state of the nation, it was impossible to plan ahead with any certainty. So most tape-recorded interviews had 'early outs', where in times of emergency the machine could be stopped and the interview ended in the middle at a point where it sounded as though it had actually finished. This was the theory, but hands can understandably be a little trembly in the early morning, and we sometimes experienced what I used to call the Morning of the Strangled Cry. You might hear an interviewer saying perhaps: 'There are three further points I would like to raise: first . . .' and then there would be a strangled cry as the tape belatedly stopped. A moment's pause, and then the solemn pronouncement: 'The time is twenty-five past eight' – and somewhere in the regions an engineer would turn a switch, a producer would sigh with relief, and a local programme would begin.

A live interview was rather more difficult to control. Our guest might be nervous at first, but a couple of minutes of Jack's genial banter would put him at ease, and by 8.24 he might be well into his stride and happy to give the nation the entire story of his life, with nothing in the world able to stop him. Green lights would start flashing all around him without the slightest effect – perhaps he thought it was Christmas. We would gesture at him, put our fingers to our lips, the producer would beat his head against the glass window, all to no avail. It seemed at times that a genuine strangled cry was the only answer. Indeed I was sometimes tempted to take advantage of our double-presenter system and suggest that one of us led the fellow out of the studio, still talking, while the other pronounced the magic formula: 'It's twenty-five past eight.' What would actually happen was that we had to interrupt him in full cry and incur charges of discourtesy and bad manners from listeners who could not know about the tyrannical opt-outs that ruled our lives.

The other side of the coin, of course, was when items ended too early, since an early opt-out was just as exasperating for the regions as a late one. There were often gaps to be filled and odd minutes to be whiled away, mostly with idle chat since the era of the newspaper misprint was to come later. Jack did occasionally quote a 'funny' from Peterborough's column in the *Daily Telegraph*, his favourite reading, but when that failed he would engage me in conversation, sometimes with remarkable results.

On one occasion 'Thought for the Day' had finished far too early; the speaker, presumably, had run out of thoughts. The topic had been 'Your favourite hymn', and when the recording ended ('Thought for the Day' is always pre-recorded, since I suspect they do not rise all that early in Religious Broadcasting) Jack noted that a minute still remained before the 7.50 opt-out. He suddenly enquired of me as the mike became live: 'Tell me John, what is *your* favourite hymn?'

As the nation held its breath for my answer the grim realisation dawned upon me that I had not the faintest idea what my favourite hymn was. For one interminable second I could think of no hymns at all, as my mind went a complete blank. Then from the dim recesses I recalled a hymn which as a schoolboy I had sung so enthusiastically at the end of term.

'Lord, dismiss us with thy blessing!' I cried.

'What a good idea,' said Jack – and left.

Thus some element of the old easy-going, unpredictable 'Today' was retained, and I hope it was never entirely lost. Jack would break all the rules of broadcasting – he would rustle his papers under the mike, he would cough and 'fluff' his way through the script, during the review of the papers he would stroll round the studio jingling the coins in his pocket and making it sound as if we were taking a collection for the newsreader, and he took a delight in the most ridiculous practical jokes. These were no longer the days when announcers set fire to one another's scripts or placed wastepaper baskets over each other's head in mid-sentence, though Jack was part of that era too. But there was one morning when we had a cageful of mice in the studio while we interviewed their owner, and when Desmond Lynam started his sports spot after the interview Jack put one of them on the poor chap's script. Like a true professional Desmond kept going magnificently, but there was an enormous grin on Jack's face, and the familiar twinkle in his eyes, as the mouse took a gentle stroll up Desmond's sleeve.

The new 'Today' was gradually taking shape. It has sometimes been called the flagship of Radio 4, but when Jack was its skipper the atmosphere was more like a cruise liner, a relaxed and escapist world. As it became more streamlined, more strongly manned and more heavily armed with the big guns from politics and industry and international affairs, this atmosphere could not always be maintained, although I hope we eventually achieved a blend of both kinds of vessel and kept a few deck games among the gun turrets. Jack, I know, did not enjoy the re-fit. He never reconciled himself to the idea of getting in at 5.30 to go through the papers, to write the links, to plan the live interviews. He never automatically followed every news bulletin to keep up with stories which he might have to report. Certainly it never occurred to him to retire early, just because he had the programme to present next day. Most of all, he disagreed with the basic principle of dual presentation, though it was more than a year after he left the programme that he publicly said so. In an interview in the *Sunday Express*, under the heading, 'Why I never listen to the Today programme', he was quoted as saying:

It is impossible for two people on sound radio to present one programme. The presenter has got to talk to the listener. He must not talk to other people in the studio and if he cracks a joke he has got to crack that joke with the chap who is going to have a shave or sitting on the lavatory or the girl who is getting the baby up . . . When I was doing it with John Timpson I found it was almost inevitable that we were talking to one another instead of to the listener. That's where I think they have gone wrong.

Although I can understand how Jack felt, later events proved that it was he who was wrong. The two-presenter style was an essential ingredient of the new 'Today' and when two people are talking in the studio the listener can always be included in the conversation.

Meanwhile there were other innovations. Instead of the occasional motoring 'flash', Douglas Cameron was given his own set times for weather and travel news, complete with temperature readings for the main cities and seasonal titbits like the final posting dates for Christmas. He was even put into a helicopter on occasions when traffic was particularly heavy, through strikes or Bank Holidays, to pick out the traffic jams and suggest diversions. I sometimes wondered if Douglas could distinguish the difference between the M1 and the Grand Union Canal from up there, but his information was always convincing and when he ran short we could always let him have more from AA headquarters which he then, just as convincingly, broadcast back. It was an old South-East Region trick, supplying reporters in the field with information to put in their on-the-spot reports, a harmless enough device by no means peculiar to the BBC.

This was not the only legacy we inherited from Marshall's days with South-East Region. A number of his reporting team came with him, among them Malcolm Billings, that most English of Australians, whose mellow clubroom voice has often shared the presentation with me, and Bob Friend, an irrepressible soul who turned in enough interviews on some mornings to fill the programme twice over. Bob is so news-prone that when he was made the BBC's first Australia correspondent, within a few months of his arrival in a country notably lacking until then in international news, Mr Stonehouse showed up in Melbourne, Darwin was devastated by a cyclone, and the Prime Minister was thrown out by the Governor General. Also from South-East Region came the incomparable Fred Streeter and his Boswell, Frank Hennig – Frank and Fred the Flowerpot Men, as Mike Aspel affectionately christened them. Another member of the 'Today' team, and by far its fittest member, was the youngest sixty-year-old in broadcasting, Eileen Fowler. For a time we also boasted the oldest twelve-year-old in broadcasting, a boy wonder called Sebastian.

Sebastian, who proved to be one of Marshall's most successful gimmicks, was brought in to conduct a course on decimalisation. Douglas Cameron played the straight man putting the questions and Sebastian provided all the answers – at least, that was how Marshall had visualised it. In practice Sebastian proved far from infallible, and it sometimes took a lot of patient tutoring by Douglas to ensure that the answers were correct, but it was an ingenious way of educating the public in the mysteries of new pence, and I suspect that Sebastian learned quite a bit too.

One other innovation affected me rather more personally. Even in his South-East Region days Marshall had had an eye for

112

international coverage. He believed firmly that the south-east included the north coast of France, or at least that part of it visible through binoculars to south-eastern listeners, and he frequently presented items from Calais or Boulogne. Now of course his empire stretched wider, and he took advantage of the two-presenter style to send half the programme abroad for the big 'set piece' occasion. Since I was the journalistic half of the presenter team it was my half that went. This was no 'fire brigade' operation, since there were studios to be arranged, lines to be booked, contacts to be made in advance. The assignments were not necessarily too disruptive, and one could generally foresee fairly accurately when the coverage would end – no Zambian-style lingering at the ringside, waiting for the action to start. Inevitably, though, because of the hours involved, they were wearying as well as predictable.

The first of our 'Euroflits', as they came to be known, was to Brussels for Mr Geoffrey Rippon's Common Market negotiations. The meetings invariably continued into the early hours, an admirable opportunity for 'Today' scoops but not too conducive to regular sleep. On our second excursion, to Luxembourg, the press conference announcing the final agreement – 'Die historische Pressekonferenz,' as the Luxembourg papers very fairly called it – took place at five in the morning, far too late for the morning papers, so my interviews with Mr Rippon and M. Schumann for the 'Today' programme were the first intimations to the British people that we were on our way into Europe.

Very typically, a 'herogram' was waiting for me when I arrived home: 'Many thanks for bringing home bacon once again.' It was one of Marshall's more endearing features that he never failed to congratulate his staff on such occasions, nor failed to pass on the congratulations of others. He rarely did it verbally, for in spite of all his drive and ambition Marshall was a shy man who preferred to put pen to paper rather than hand on shoulder. The office was regularly showered with memos 'To all "Today" Staff', and I often felt Marshall did not have a tea-break, he had a memo-pause. At least it did mean that we knew what was going on in the higher echelons, what future plans might be, what was thought of the plans we had tried so far. It was a fairly basic exercise in man management, but not every manager of men troubles to do it.

113

One other event in that first twelve months turned out rather less pleasantly. Early in 1971 I went down with appendicitis. The operation was successful, but the day after I returned home I was whisked back to hospital with a pulmonary embolism, a rather unpleasant condition involving a blood clot which might have landed up in some fairly fatal places. Happily it was dispersed successfully, but I was on anti-coagulants, and the waggon, for some time afterwards, and it gave us all a rather nasty scare. However, it had its compensations. Good wishes came in from all sorts of kindly strangers, I could listen to the programme in bed for a change, and while I was convalescing we took the chance of doing some house-hunting. In due course we moved to a fresh home in Chorleywood, only half a mile from our previous one but rather roomier and with its own built-in Fred Streeter, a genial aged retainer called Mr Parrott who looked after the garden.

Marshall was also taking his opportunities, and two new presenters were tried out while I was away – an up-and-coming Northerner called Michael Parkinson, then presenting a rather obscure film programme on ITV, and Joan Bakewell, one of the 'Line-Up' team from BBC2. Marshall always had an eye for the television name, but found to his cost that sometimes a sparkling personality on the screen can be a terrible drag on radio. Joan Bakewell was the first woman to present the 'Today' programme, but like others who followed her, her stay was brief. Mike also moved on fairly promptly, in his case to conquer rather different fields.

It was interesting to read the press comments about these changes. There was for instance Gillian Reynolds in the *Guardian*; I wonder if she could have visualised then that five years later she would have a chance to present the 'Today' programme herself – the first 'Today' poacher to turn gamekeeper, though she might see it the other way.

To be sure [she wrote] Messrs Cameron and Parkinson were brisk, incisive, well-tempered and evenly matched. With them 'Today' sounded like everything was going to plan or even better. What one missed, however, was the atmosphere of the unexpected which Mr de Manio manages so unfailingly to create . . . He makes me cross and even occasionally despair, but he also makes me aware that this is live radio. 'Today' presented by Messrs Timpson and de Manio represents the world of the conserved middle class and has a storybook charm of its own. 'Today' presented by Messrs Cameron and Parkinson sounded like a news magazine and, dear knows, there are enough of them about on Radio 4 already.

That apparently kindly comment may actually have helped Jack towards the door. In the view of our masters there was still a little too much of the 'storybook charm', not enough of the news magazine. When I was asked to give my choice of programmes for *Radio Times* I tried to redress the balance with a word about the value and the speed of radio news and current affairs on programmes like ours 'and that daily miracle, "The World at One." How do they manage to fill twenty minutes each lunchtime with what is left after "Today"?' It prompted a pat on the back from Peter Woon, and a few dark looks from 'The World at One', but the decision about the future of the 'Today' presenters had I think already been made. Whether, as one paper speculated, Jack jumped or whether he was pushed was never

Two eras merge: Jack de Manio, Robert Robinson, John Timpson and Douglas Cameron make their only joint appearance, for a New Year's Eve programme to welcome 1972. [BBC *Copyright*]

115

entirely clear, but in April 1971, just a year after our partnership began, the news broke of his departure. It was thought by some that there would be a public outcry, that listeners would not tolerate 'Today' without him, but the public's memory is short and fans can be fickle. Within a few weeks the letters of protest stopped arriving, within a few months his name was rarely mentioned in connection with the programme, and a few years later many people seemed to have forgotten that he had ever had anything to do with it.

Yet in his way Jack provided a breakthrough in broadcasting techniques just as revolutionary as all the much-vaunted Sounds of the Seventies put together. He was the first broadcaster to get away successfully from the traditional BBC image of neutral impersonality and to behave on the air like the genial, fallible fellow he really was. For those twelve years millions of listeners looked on him as a personal friend – exasperating sometimes, as friends can be, but always a genuine, reassuring, three-dimensional figure at their breakfast table, and great company. They could keep in touch with him of course through his new afternoon programme, 'Jack de Manio Precisely', and I hope he enjoyed its relaxed atmosphere more than the increasing pressures of 'Today'. His departure from peak-time broadcasting was the most significant feature yet of radio's new approach to current affairs, and if ever an era had an ending, that was it.

Speculation about his successor ranged from Michael Parkinson to Simon Dee, but Marshall had laid his plans shrewdly. In a blaze of publicity, which only he could have engineered, the new presenter was revealed as a man already well known on television for 'Call My Bluff', 'The Fifties', 'Points of View' and 'Ask the Family', but never heard regularly before on radio. Into Jack's shoes stepped Robert Robinson, as different from Jack as a wire-haired terrier is from and old English sheepdog. On his first day on the programme a telegram arrived from the old maestro to the new one: 'Wishing you great success. Don't, repeat don't, give up booze or go to bed early unless absolutely worthwhile, otherwise life becomes hell.' It was a fair summary of Jack's philosophy, and an appropriate farewell.

Chapter Thirteen

Bringing Robert Robinson into the 'Today' team was a gamble. Nobody could know whether listeners would tolerate the company at breakfast-time of an intellect so lively and at times so exhausting. As well as that, it was Bob's first experience of a programme like ours, and it was my first experience of Bob. We had never met before, and we could quite easily have taken an instant dislike to one another and turned the programme into a breakfast brawl. But like most of Marshall's gambles it turned out to be a winner, and the original trial period of three months extended eventually into three years.

On the face of it we made an unlikely pair. Bob was an Oxford man, a star of the Union in the vintage years of Shirley Williams, Norman St John Stevas and the rest; in those years I was reporting garden fetes and church bazaars around the obscurer corners of the Harrow Road, and my only union activities were in the NUJ. During that period Bob learned to use words to fashion lexicological objets d'art; I learned to use them just to convey information. Now Bob lived in a period town house in Chelsea with a weekend cottage in Somerset, belonged to a good club and knew his way round the more exclusive restaurants and the finer cellars of the West End; I continued to enjoy the semi-rural, semi-suburban life of Chorleywood, I was often unnerved by head waiters and I hardly knew a Beaune from a Beaujolais. We lived in completely different worlds among completely different people, and this was perhaps why our early-morning camaraderie endured so well: we were never in each other's company long enough to get on each other's nerves. The programme was our main common interest, and it gave us scope to exercise one other common factor, a sense of humour – or more accurately, an appreciation of the ridiculous. We rarely met outside the studio during the three years we worked together, and since then we have met hardly at all.

If I had qualms about working with a man of such different talents and background, Bob had his as well. He made them clear in his interviews with the Press. 'I've never been up earlier than 9.30 since I did my National Service,' he told them. 'I don't know whether I shall be fluent at that time of day.' And after his first programme he told the London *Evening News*: 'I was absolutely ravaged by nerves. You've got no idea how brutally spontaneous it all is. I was appalled by everyone's calmness – I was fluttering like a lavendered old lady.'

The fluttering soon ceased, and as for his fluency, it never deserted him either on or off the air. The 'Today' team spent many memorable breakfasts after the programme listening to his astonishing flow of elegant multiloquence. I have known him to be stopped in his tracks only once, and not by any Cicero of the cornflakes. The credit went to Gloria, our West Indian cleaner, who 'did us out' at breakfast-time and was virtually a member of the team herself. Gloria was listening to Bob one morning, like the rest of us, open-mouthed. A moment came when he paused for breath after a particularly dazzling burst of Augustan prose, and in the silence came Gloria's fruity Jamaican voice. 'Mr Rarbinson,' she said, 'you bin drinkin' again!'

Surprisingly perhaps, Bob's verbal pyrotechnics in the early morning proved an instant success. As with any success, there were the carpers; the *Daily Mirror*, for instance, compared Robert (Smarty) Robinson with Jack (Cosy) de Manio, both descriptions being equally inaccurate. Mary Griffiths wrote of Bob's 'battering-ram personality', but then she described me as 'a teacher-like figure', which was even more fanciful. It was she, incidentally, who called Bob the hare of the programme and me the tortoise. It seemed a bit insulting at the time, except that she added 'We know who wins in the end'. As it turned out, we both won. The combination seemed to go down well with the vast majority of our listeners, and gradually the new 'Today' took shape. The programme hardened, in more than one sense, in the mould that Marshall had cast. The team of reporters and producers quarried for the nuggets throughout the night and cut them into shape and balance, then Bob and I tried to provide the final polish and create the appropriate setting. On some mornings the stones were so lustreless that no amount of polishing could make them shine; on many others, Bob's links were so dazzling in themselves that they outshone the stones. Usually, though, we managed to thread everything together so that all the different facets combined to give an overall sparkle to the morning.

Under Bob's hand the thirty-second cue became a new art form. Even when I could not follow precisely what he was talking about, the words made a delightful pattern of their own. Any visiting pundit was no longer asked to speculate, he was invited to 'cast the runes'; an introduction to some worthy but unexciting discussion on the economy would be embellished with a homily from Horace or a Balzacian bon mot; and I loved to watch a guest's eyes glaze over as one of Bob's questions developed clauses and sub-clauses of Homeric proportions. He could be devastating in debate, but never tried to score off an inexperienced interviewee, and was kindness itself to anyone overawed by the studio surroundings or indeed by Bob himself. He also had some very set ideas on how the programme should be introduced. He would never accept the custom of announcing his own name, and I know he disapproved of my regular greeting, 'A very good morning to you', as being over-effusive and unnecessary. He

The 'Today' studio during the Robert Robinson era. With the two 'Today' presenters is the late Douglas Smith, one of the better-known newsreaders who joined us to read the review of the morning papers. [*Syndication International*]

never actually told me so, and it was after he had left that I was shown a letter he had written to a listener who also objected to the phrase and asked him to correct me. 'How could I do that to a fellow toiler in the vineyard?' he had replied. 'It would be like telling a chap he was dropping his aitches.'

The third member of the presentation team, Douglas Cameron, proved the ideal 'straight man' and stood up gamely to a fair amount of ribbing over his weather and travel reports, although sometimes our exchanges backfired. There was, for instance, the Great Blubberhouses Controversy, which nearly precipitated another civil war and set the dalesmen of Yorkshire on the march to Broadcasting House. Douglas came in one morning with his customary announcement, 'I've just had a flash!' ('He looks all right to me,' Bob would mutter) It appeared that there was dense fog at somewhere called Blubberhouses, a name completely new to me and with a certain fairy-tale flavour to it. There were a few seconds to spare, so I idly observed that it seemed improbable such a name could really exist. Immediately switchboards were jammed, letterboxes were filled and the air over the Ridings became blue as half the population of Yorkshire bombarded us with information about Blubberhouses. I was sent descriptions of it, photographs of it, maps of it, the history of it, all accompanied by scandalised references to my southern stupidity. Local papers took up the attack, and as a side issue a long correspondence ensued about the origin of the name. The most romantic suggestion was that small children were forced to work in the mill there, and their 'blubbering' could be heard across the moors. A connection was suggested with the whaling industry, not too likely for a village fifty-odd miles inland, and 'blubber' was variously interpreted as a sheep, a spring and a berry. It all got a tremendous amount of publicity, and Marshall was quite delighted, but it was some time before I dared visit Yorkshire again.

One other casual remark to Douglas got me in hot water too. He was talking about congestion, a subject always dear to his heart, and he mentioned Scots Hill in Rickmansworth. This was one of the few occasions that Douglas mentioned anywhere I had ever heard of (I often wondered if he invented some of these congested areas, just to keep things going), and I pressed him for further details. He advised me that a lorry had shed its load – a quaint expression used by traffic buffs to indicate that the stuff had fallen off the back – and it appeared that there were fifteen hundred tins of corned beef all over Scots Hill.

'My word,' I cried, 'my house is just round the corner from Scots Hill. I must ring home and get the kids out with a barrow'.

Within seconds the phone in the office was ringing. 'Tell John Timpson,' said the lady, 'it is quite disgusting to encourage his children to steal food off the road!'

Fortunately our studio banter was not always taken so seriously. As the months went by we became fairly well prepared for each other's impromptu observations and the 'Today' programme developed its own brand of good humour, in both senses. Sometimes we incorporated it in our cues, and since we had copies of each other's scripts we were able to prepare a suitable riposte, but generally the comments merely arose as we went along. If a Robinsonian sally could cause a razor to slip in some distant bathroom, it could also prove disconcerting in the studio, particularly if a certain solemnity was required to introduce, for instance, 'Thought for the Day'.

Meanwhile Marshall was still dreaming up new ideas and extending his empire. An extra fifteen minutes was added to the programme, which was started at 6.45 instead of seven, and a late-night 'trail' was introduced, giving details of the items we hoped to have next morning; it could have been listened to only by insomniacs and mariners awaiting the shipping forecast, but it was another little segment of broadcasting territory which now bore the 'Today' flag. We also took over the New Year spot on Radio 4, with a programme around midnight which was memorable only for the 'live' row on the air between Bob and Lord Longford whom he introduced, following his anti-pornography campaign, as the Lost Cause of the Year.

The most spectacular development was to expand our outside broadcast activities. There were the marathon Euroflits when we joined the Common Market and on the anniversaries that followed, a week of programmes presented from a different European city each morning, with Bob and myself, each accompanied by a producer, leapfrogging each other around the Community in a blur of different studios, different languages, and different problems with the local communication systems. We would land in a new city with a handful of telephone numbers and a case of blank tapes, and spend hours in hotel bedrooms contacting politicians and journalists and local

121

dignitaries, anyone who could speak a little English. We would dash off in taxis to record interviews and 'atmosphere' and 'What do you think of Britain in the Community?', then stay up into the early hours writing scripts and editing tape and phoning London to plan out the programme. After perhaps a couple of hours' sleep, it is off to the studios of ORTF or RAI or Radio Norge to try to explain in French or Italian or pidgin-Norwegian when the tapes should be played and when the mike should be live, what an opt-out is, and why we have to hear London as well as London hearing us. The programme itself is two hours of impromptu hand-signals as lights fail to work, of frenzied phone calls as lines go down, and of sheer panic as interviewees fail to appear, or a tape goes on backwards, or a script is lost and we cannot explain to our baffled technicians what is wrong. Somehow it all comes right in the end, and we stumble out of the studio, get a cab to the airport and, as the plane takes off, open a new folder marked Hamburg or Dublin or Brussels.

It says much for the patience and skill of our broadcasting colleagues all over Europe that of all the many programmes we presented from there I remember only one where we went off the air for a few moments because a line was shut instead of open, and only one other where the wrong voice was heard because a line was open instead of shut. Otherwise, whether we were in the ageing but cosy studios of Radio Belge, the gleaming new studios of Radio Hilversum, or our own shoe-cupboard of a studio in Paris, the programmes always got through. I hope they gave some coherent impression of the country we were in and the people we were among. The only impression I ever retained after a week of Euroflitting was a cosmopolitan hotch-potch of interviewing skiers in Oslo and pilgrims in Rome, of Fanny Blankers-Koen in Amsterdam delving into a wardrobe to find me her Olympic gold medal, of Sir Christopher Soames in his Paris Embassy plying us with Scotch, of the cinema in Copenhagen which showed 'Snow White and the Seven Dwarfs' in the afternoon and 'Deep Throat' in the evening, of one New Year's Eve spent dancing a conga with the Norwegian equivalent of the Townswomen's Guild because their party was the only place in town we could get a drink, and of another spent on the notorious Reeperbahn, slumped over a chop-suey in an entirely innocuous Chinese restaurant because we were too weary to sample anything else. Always there was the common denominator of the hotel bedroom with the typewriter on the dressing-table, the recorder on the bed and discarded tape all over the floor.

Not all our excursions were quite so hectic. We spent periods of up to a week in New York for the presidential and mid-term elections, a couple of rather less restful periods in Belfast when internment was introduced and when the cease-fire was declared, and a rather jolly weekend in Edinburgh for the Festival. Because of his other commitments in television Bob generally stayed in the studio while I took my half of the programme on tour, whether it was to Paris for a summit meeting or to Westminster Abbey for Princess Anne's wedding – an interesting feat, incidentally, to present half a programme from a deserted Abbey about a wedding which had not even started. It all prompted the *Guardian* to refer to me rather charmingly as 'setting out from Portland Place, a pocket handkerchief on the end of a stick over the shoulder, off to seek the Holy Scoop'.

Probably the most arduous of these sorties, and the least rewarding in terms of duty-free Scotch and cigars, were the party conferences. I had been attending these strange tribal ceremonies, a cross between an old boys' reunion and a medieval bearfight, since 1960, first as a 'legman' running errands for the Parliamentary correspondents, then to present a round-up of each day's events for the 'Ten O'Clock' programme including live interviews with delegates in various stages of 'exhaustion'. Now I covered them for 'Today'. Each party has achieved its own conference ambience over the years: the Liberals are cheerful, charming and frequently, thanks to the Young Liberals, confused; Labour are outwardly convivial, privately cantankerous and, when it's time for *Auld Lang Syne*, embarrassingly comradely; and the Conservatives remain ostentatiously composed, contented and just a tiny bit condescending.

It is difficult, looking back, to tell one year from another. The most memorable I attended was at Scarborough in 1960, the year of the great Labour division over Clause Four. I was reminded of it when I went back there fifteen years later for the Liberal Assembly, the only party now compact enough to use the Scarborough facilities. The Spa Pavilion was quite unchanged, with Max Jaffa still playing there as he did in 1960. The radio and television caravans were outside on the promenade again, and the BBC's temporary offices were up in the roof garden over the heads of the delegates (one producer said to me, as the sun poured in through the glass roof, 'By the end of the week we'll have grown three inches and be putting out shoots!') There was the same cliff path with the delegates walking down from the hotels above, and it was very easy, instead of those 1975 Liberals, to picture the burly figure of Frank Cousins and his union colleagues, and the frailer figure of Hugh Gaitskell and his more moderate supporters, making their way into the great debate which produced that remarkable cry of defiance from the party leader: 'I shall fight, and fight, and fight again to save the party that I love.' I have heard many fine conference speeches and many fine orators, but all too often one feels that the more dramatic the speech, the louder the orator, the less is actually being said. I have heard none more effective, more genuine and more moving than Hugh Gaitskell that day.

However cynical one may get about motives and manoeuvrings at these conferences, they have a rather special atmosphere which one cannot help absorb, not only in the conference hall but in the corridors, the hotels, the foyers and the bars. Nationally known figures congregate under one seaside roof, the political correspondents huddle in corners noting which cocktail parties are being attended by which leaders and who is being ostracised by whom, and who knows which Secretary of State may share your lift, or what Cabinet Minister may be using the next stall?

During the major conferences we have taken a 'Today' team to the conference town and presented half the programme from there throughout the week. It has not always been easy to fill that half, since even the most politically minded listener can weary of party squabbles, real or manufactured. For the Liberals and the TUC we have lately limited coverage to a one-day operation, on the opening morning of the conference, presenting all the major figures and the main topics of debate and thus pre-empting, we rather hope, most of our current affairs colleagues.

Even with these one-day spectaculars we have tried to leaven the political loaf with more yeasty material from the conference fringes. Thus at Blackpool we visited the Milk Marketing Council's butter-making display on the promenade, where a charming milkmaid taught me how to churn butter: 'And stop it!' she cried as I grunted over the churn, 'and stop it! and stop it!' Heaven knows what speculation that aroused among listeners who tuned in late. At Scarborough we chatted with Max Jaffa, who literally shared the bill at the Spa, since his signature is permanently emblazoned on the curtain above the speakers' heads. We even took a ride on an imported Parisian bus in one conference town, since its destination board, Place de Clichy, sounded most appropriate for political oratory.

The 'Today' team prepare for a little traditional first-footing to welcome 1974. [*Radio Times*]

In the main our combination of the serious with the light relief, not just at conferences but in the programme as a whole, seemed to suit our breakfast-time audience fairly well. Within the BBC, commendations came from the governors, from directors and controllers, not least from the late Tony Whitby, Controller of Radio 4 and the man largely responsible for encouraging Marshall to develop the new 'Today'. Audience research produced encouraging statistics about listening figures and audience appreciation, and the Radio Industries Club named 'Today' as the radio programme of the year – after year, after year.

Behind all these moments of glory there was the relentless routine of the 4.30 reveille which continued morning after morning, whether it was to be a day of drama and urgency or one of those programmes euphemistically known as 'worthy' – mornings when Bob and I were known to the team as the Brothers Grimm as we waded through a gloomy swampland of industrial disputes and the decaying economy and a plummeting pound. Each morning was unpredictable, with no hint of what awaited us as we entered the office at 5.30, nor what hazards might arise once the programme began. It was this constant element of the unexpected, the hope that this would be the Big One, that made the tedious preliminaries worthwhile.

The routine for these preliminaries, as far as I am concerned, has developed such a precise pattern that any self-respecting robot could be programmed to do it, from the moment the first alarm clock explodes at 4.30 (another is set for five minutes later, in case the first one fails). First the blunder through the darkness to the bedroom door, to a mumbled farewell from under the bedclothes as Pat tries to regain unconsciousness, sometimes successfully, but on a restless morning it is out with the ironing-board to pass the time until breakfast. Such are the unappreciated repercussions of 'unsocial hours'. Into the bathroom and the glare of electric light and the deafening buzz of the razor. Only once did I venture to the office unshaven. It had been a late night, I was up a little later and moving a little slower and after all, I thought, this is radio. I was not to know that on that particular morning we had a brigadier to interview, a most charming man but still a brigadier. I just caught his glance at my stubbly chin, and I never appeared in the studio unshaven again. At one stage I did grow a beard, in the hope of saving a few precious minutes in the morning, but it turned out to be rather raggety and very grey, the sort you see on a cattle rustler in a second-rate Western. After a decent period it came off, to become a lasting source of confusion in my passport.

The bathroom is also the dressing room, with the clothes distributed around the walls in precisely the same order each morning: shirt and tie on the towel rail, socks and pants on the laundry basket, suit hanging up behind the door, car keys in the medicine cabinet next to the after-shave. The whole dressing process is carried out on automatic pilot, and if I have forgotten to undo a top shirt-button the night before I can struggle blindly inside it for interminable seconds with arms flailing helplessly in the air. At that hour tying a shoelace can be as complex as crochet, inserting a cufflink needs the skill of a surgeon.

Now down the stairs, avoiding the creaky one, pick up the briefcase in the hall, use the key to shut the front door behind me to prevent it slamming, and into the car for the twenty-five miles to Broadcasting House. In a few hours' time the road will be clogged at every cross roads and roundabout, but now it is a commuter's paradise, a deserted highway where foxes still safely roam. The few other travellers are almost old friends – the same rogue newspaper van belting along the fast lane, the same old butcher's van ambling along the slow one, the same little man on the pavement with the flat cap and the umbrella at the slope, giving you a wave as he heads for goodness knows where. Each morning he waves and I dip my lights, and other drivers dip theirs – thank heaven, the spirit of the Railway Children lives on. In the summer the sun is already up and it can often be the best part of the day. In the winter, with overnight fog and a heavy frost, or perhaps with snow still lying deep and treacherous before the sweepers are out, it can often be the worst. But that half-hour or so on the road each morning is invaluable for letting the mind tick over and gently warm up before arriving in the office and crashing immediately into top gear.

It is at the office that the real effort begins. As people often point out, there is nothing unique about getting up early: bakers do it, and postmen, and market porters and the rest. But bakers do not have to grasp the latest report of the Organisation of Economic and Cultural Development at 5.30 in the morning, postmen do not have to interview a particularly devious union leader before breakfast about his latest strike call, market porters do not have to devise an entertaining way of introducing a man who shows sex films to polar bears, or a centenarian who owes it all to clean living, hard work and eating six chrysanthemums a day. Having done that, none of them has to be civil to seven million people.

The hour before the programme provides the real test, and the real reward. Check through the running order to see which topics we shall be handling, what new developments have happened overnight and whom we shall be interviewing, have ten minutes with the morning papers, skimming through the news pages and accumulating extra titbits which may be of use in a cue or as a filler, then off to the typewriter and those sheets of ominously blank paper. Bob and I would sit opposite each other, staring into space, sometimes for minutes on end, as the right phrase refused to come. What is there left to say about redundancies in the steel industry? How can you sum up the current political situation in Portugal in twenty-five seconds? Surely we interviewed the chairman of the Kidderminster Kipper Club only last week? Gradually the words come, not always the right words, but linger any longer and we shall still be writing when we should be in the studio. Indeed, on many mornings the final cues are still being written during the weather forecast or the sports news or 'Thought for the Day'. Around us the night reporters and producers are still editing tape and phoning Sydney or Buenos Aires, and the night editor is still searching the agency tapes for a late story or rousing politicians from their beds to persuade them into the studio. Meanwhile Bob passes another mini-masterpiece to the secretaries to duplicate, and at last I think of a comment about the research unit which has found that cheese cleans teeth better than toothpaste – 'the only place in the country where the mice have a ring of confidence'.

Sixty seconds to go and we are off to the studio with our bundle of scripts and cuttings and questions; a quick greeting to the newsreader and the production team behind the window, and it is 6.45. 'A very good morning to you from the "Today" team. First the news headlines . . .' and away we go on our two-hour tightrope. On a bad morning the balance can be all wrong; the programme may sink into stodginess, or we may over-compensate and become too facetious. There may be too many economists and social reformers, or too many flagpole-sitters and players on the bones. Sometimes the mixture is just right: the big news story that broke too late for the papers, the genuine eccentric with an entertaining tale to tell, the studio interview that suddenly sparks into life, the impromptu observation that makes even the producer laugh. These are the moments which make the 'Today' programme exciting to work for, because you never know when they will arise. Nor can you foresee the hazards: the last-minute changes, the sudden live telephone-call with no time for a preliminary chat, cutting the cues and the tapes as we go along to fit in the extra story, the guest who will not stop talking and the one with absolutely nothing to say, the circuit that fails to come up, the tape that inexplicably breaks. In the middle of all of this we have to make it sound as if it has all been planned long beforehand and we are just enjoying a leisurely breakfast with some interesting people. Perhaps we have won when listeners say 'But what actual *work* do you do, the rest of the day?'

Chapter Fourteen

The 'actual work' that I did, for the rest of most days, was limited to keeping up with the 'Today' correspondence and other paperwork until lunchtime, either in the office or at my own desk at home, then catching up on my sleep in the afternoon. When people constantly ask 'How do you manage to get up in the mornings?' this is the simple answer, although other presenters, including Bob, have not found it quite so simple. It involves re-gearing the metabolism and re-adjusting life as a whole to fit in with the double-bedtime routine, and unless one is prepared to accept this, and one's family is prepared to accept it too, then no average constitution is likely to survive for very long, certainly not for year after year. The alternative is to turn in by nine o'clock each evening, an even more anti-social arrangement with even less chance of any normal family life.

As it was, Pat and I worked out a tolerable routine. I worked in the morning, we had a pleasant lunch together, then I retired to bed – causing a few nudges among the neighbours when they saw the bedroom curtains drawn every afternoon. We eventually convinced our friends that the telephone bell and the front-door knocker would not disturb me, after Pat had endured a period of almost complete isolation when nobody would call or phone in case they woke me, and when commuters were coming home from work and the boys were coming home from school I was coming down the stairs, able to spend the evening with the family until a civilised hour. It was tempting sometimes to lunch too lavishly to ensure a sound afternoon sleep, which in turn could mean a thick head at teatime, and on those rare weekdays when we went out to dinner this could add up to two hangovers a day. In general, though, the system worked well and if I varied it too often I soon felt the effects.

I did manage to fit in some other BBC work, though nothing on the scale of Bob's other activities. There was a most enjoyable six months, for instance, presenting the 'After Seven' programme on Radio 2, an hour of pleasant music and amiable chat, with complete freedom to make any observations which came to mind, and a great chance to use the fillers we had no room for at breakfast-time. No races between the opt-outs, no pontificating politicians or dismal doomwatchers, just a relaxing escapist hour on a Monday evening with still a fair audience around as folk ate their dinner or completed a long drive home. We even presented a Paris edition one week, when it coincided with a State Visit I was covering for 'Today'. 'Who would have thought,' wrote the *Guardian* (which I have quoted so frequently because, to their shame, few other newspapers run a regular radio column) 'that stern old television newscasting John Timpson could have broken through into a whole new light-hearted role in radio?' I hope almost anyone who knew me would have thought so, but as it turned out, it was made discreetly clear that a 'Today' presenter should not be a disc-jockey in his spare time, even in the rather gentle Seekers-and-Sinatra atmosphere of 'After Seven'.

My extra-mural work therefore had to remain on a more serious plane, and this led me logically into the realms of further education. I presented a number of FE programmes on television: 'People Ltd', a series about the human side of big organisations, 'Life in the Nine', about the European Community, and 'Out of the Rut', ten programmes about changing jobs in mid-career. Further education does not command peak viewing time; the programmes seemed to go out either at midday or midnight, and while they were running people were still asking me why I never did any television, but the production team put tremendous effort into them. I learned a lot from them, not least how to behave in a television studio when you can actually get up and walk about, a process quite unknown in Television News and involving, unlike newsreading, wearing trousers which actually match the jacket.

'Out of the Rut' presented a further problem, in that it had to be recorded in Manchester, for administrative reasons which have baffled better men than me. Bryn Brooks and Anna Jackson, the producer and director, would travel up the previous day and I would catch a train after the 'Today' programme to arrive at lunchtime; we would rehearse and record during the afternoon and early evening and catch the 8.10 back to town, with a BBC picnic dinner in lieu of a restaurant car. My double-sleep system collapsed completely on such days, and it fared little better when Douglas Smith, a former news cameraman now producing regional programmes in Leeds, invited me to present some programmes from the Leeds studio. This involved travelling to Leeds after 'Today', snatching a couple of hours' sleep in a hotel during the afternoon, recording the programme in the evening and returning to town on the overnight sleeper, stumbling out of King's Cross station and into the 'Today' office at five o'clock next morning. But the programmes were great fun to do and well worth all the upheaval: there was a Northern 'Gardeners' Question Time', a television version of the radio series with the same cheery trio arguing about potash and greenfly and how to grow a privet hedge in a windowbox; and a sort of curators' quiz, called 'The Object in Question', where various northern museums tried to baffle each other with mystery objects from their collections, perhaps a niddy noddy or a dame's clicker or an apothecary's corker. Both series seemed to me well worth a national showing, as indeed so many regional productions do; certainly among their regional audience they proved a success.

One other regional programme gave me particular pleasure. Douglas Salmon, television producer in Norwich, invited me to appear in his 'In Camera' series, and for half an hour I took the interviewee's chair for a change and was allowed to talk my head off about the life and times of John Timpson – to me a most fascinating subject. Tony Scase was the unfortunate interviewer, who I gather had prepared a whole fistful of penetrating questions and managed to get in only about the first three. I am not sure what the viewers thought, but I enjoyed it tremendously.

I was given a similar opportunity on radio, but in rather less complimentary circumstances. The producer of Pete Murray's 'Open House' programme rang the 'Today' office in desperation one morning: a studio guest had failed to appear, he had to fill the gap in the next ten minutes, and could Robert Robinson possibly step in? Robert decided he could not: reading record requests for amorous couples in Peckham was not, he felt, quite his line.

A note of hysteria could be detected at the other end of the phone. 'Who else is about?' they cried.

'Well,' we told them diffidently, 'there's John Timpson.'

A long pause, then they recovered magnificently. 'How absolutely splendid,' they said. 'Do ask him to come down.'

So I did, and very congenial it turned out to be. Pete and I had not met before, but he handles his programme and his guests so amiably that even if I had not enjoyed talking about myself anyway, he would soon have convinced me. I had my handwriting interpreted by Fraser White: the way I dotted my 'i's' apparently showed my natural wit and humour, the simplification of the letters confirmed my analytical mind, the shape of the 'd' indicated an interest in cultural subjects, and my lower loops showed I could control my passions. All of this seemed the right sort of thing to say about a 'Today' presenter, particularly the controlled passions, since there is little scope for unleashing them when one has to rise at 4.30 each morning. I even enjoyed reading the requests, which were rather charming and, slightly to my surprise, completely genuine. I had often wondered whether such programmes have to top up their correspondence themselves on a quiet day, but there they all were, those postcards with the picture of Shanklin beach and the names all obscured by the postmark, just like they always say.

It was this appearance on 'Open House', I gather, which caught the ears of the Light Entertainment moguls of Radio 2 and led later to my being invited to chair the quiz series, 'What's It All About?' No threat to credibility here – if Richard Dimbleby could chair 'Twenty Questions' this made the whole quiz scene respectable. They also asked me to be the anchorman in the studio for a once-only revival of 'In Town Tonight', an hour of unashamed nostalgia as once again we stopped the mighty roar of London's traffic to bring together some of the interesting people who were in town tonight. It was most notable for the revival of the two famous features of the old programme: Brian Johnston, now retired, came back for his 'Let's Go Somewhere' spot, in this case a sauna bath complete with cry of agony under the cold shower, and John Ellison returned to interview passers-by in Piccadilly Circus, as he had done for so many Saturday nights. John had been away from the microphone for eighteen months through serious illness, and this turned out to be his final broadcast; he died shortly afterwards. I was fortunate to have that chance of working with John and Brian, two masters of live broadcasting, and I took it not at all unkindly when I heard that there had been criticism of the anchorman as being an anachronism in such distinguished and veteran company. In comparison, even after sixteen years of broadcasting, I was still very much a new boy.

'Living Decisions' provided some rather more serious radio

appearances, twenty-six of them altogether, in a further education series which carried the ultimate accolade of a GCE 'O' level in 'Community and Family Studies'. It was basically how to use logical reasoning to make a decision, even if it was just where to go for a holiday or what to have for dinner. To build up this simple idea into a 26-programme series, complete with an imaginary family to perform the situations, an accompanying textbook to provide the homework and an examination to achieve an 'O' level certificate was an astonishing feat of ingenuity in itself. Full marks to the producer, Graham Tayar, who achieved it. Since my duties were largely confined to reading Graham's scripts, plus the statutory interview with Mrs Margaret Powell, without which no further education programme is complete, I did not become as deeply involved as perhaps I should have done, and I fear that if they had set me the exam at the end of the series I would have failed it comprehensively.

While this extra work within the BBC cropped up only spasmodically, there was another spare-time activity which built up into something of a cottage industry. Ever since my days with the 'royals' I had been giving talks to local Townswomen's Guilds and Women's Institutes – it was said in the office that if they banged a spoon on the table I would jump up and sing 'Jerusalem' – and now I entered a new league where the sight of a man in a red coat and white gloves would start me off for forty minutes. I was recruited by Foyles to join their troupe of performing speakers on the Luncheon Club circuit.

As a speaker's secretary in Round Table it had never occurred to me actually to pay my speakers. We serenely assumed that a pint of beer, a leg of chicken and a hearty round of applause was ample compensation for travelling miles, being polite for two or three hours to a group of complete strangers, and probably sacrificing the only free evening of the week. Many speakers of course came to publicise and to 'soft sell' as part of their normal job or on behalf of some charity, but I blush now to remember the busy, talented people whom I asked to give up their precious spare time, and who were too polite or too good-natured to say no. These days even Round Table, that most careful of organisations, recognises that the professional communicator is worthy of his hire, and while there are the philanthropic amateurs who are prepared to turn out just for the love of it, most regular speakers on the luncheon and after-dinner circuit consider it a branch of their professional activities. Unless some personal interest or charity is involved they expect to be paid accordingly.

This has of course led to moments of embarrassment, and every speaker must have his own horror story. Richard Whitmore told me that on one occasion, while still prominently placed on the platform, he was paid his fee in ten-pence pieces out of an old biscuit-tin. Lynda Lee-Potter tells of the chairman who introduced her thus: 'Miss Lee-Potter once said in her column that she never wrote anything unless she got paid for it. Well, she never says anything unless she gets paid for it either, and we'll be paying her later.' For myself, I remember the genial drunk who said, when somebody asked me if I enjoyed these visits, 'Of course he enjoys them – he gets paid for them, doesn't he?' It was one rare occasion when a reply occurred to me at the time instead of next morning. 'I am paid to make the speech,' I said coldly. 'I am civil for nothing.'

Happily such moments seldom occur. Most treasurers these days are masters of the discreet envelope, and most chairmen are courteous enough to behave like a host rather than a ringmaster. My colleagues in the 'Today' team marvel at my enthusiasm as I set out for a drive to Devizes or an Inter-City to Leicester with my speaker's emergency pack – battery razor to smarten up, alarm clock to wake up at the right station or after a nap in a lay-by and hip-flask to warm up – but I still enjoy my 'gigs', as they call them. Each audience has its own character and presents its own problems, and each occasion is a new challenge.

I started with the local Townswomen's Guilds and WIs in the early sixties, and they are still the most friendly and responsive audiences, although these days it is more often the group meeting or the federation conference rather than the individual Institute or Guild. Sometimes the chairman calls you John Simpson and it turns out that the proposer of the vote of thanks is the only member in the hall who has never heard of 'Today', and often they will apologise in advance for old Mrs X in the front row who always drops off during the talk and is liable to snore during questions. These are only minor problems though, and indeed a challenge in themselves; if the chairman gets my name right when I leave, and if the lady with the vote of thanks decides to listen to 'Today' next morning, and if I can keep old Mrs X awake for the full fifty minutes, then I feel I have won.

It has been fascinating, as a regular visitor, to watch the image of the WI and the TG change over the years and become younger and more sophisticated. The old 'jam and Jerusalem' approach is not forgotten, and I have judged many an embroidered bookmark and eaten many a home-made scone, but even in isolated little villages I find they often serve sherry before the meeting and a glass of wine with the refereshments, and one or two slightly risqué stories which I used to reserve for Round Tables now go down remarkably well with WIS. The most convincing evidence that WI can now stand for 'With It' was in a competition I judged at a meeting of the Beacon Group in Buckinghamshire. Members had to compose a telegram in which the words began with the letters of the Group's title, and I just had to award first prize to the one which read: 'Baby Expected At Christmas – Olive Now Getting Rid Of Unreliable Pills'. The fact that one of the WI dignitaries on the platform happened to be called Olive made it all the more delightful.

We have always tried to give these women's organisations a fair hearing on 'Today'. Certainly we have interviewed successive national presidents and discussed the movements' attitudes to various topics, from abortion to whether 'Jerusalem' should be dropped from WI meetings (as the only male singer on many occasions among hundreds of women, and facing them at that, it can be quite an ordeal, but the overall effect can be pretty impressive too). We did however run into trouble in one programme over a Kent village called Loose, where of course they have the Loose Women's Institute. This seemed rather funny at the time, but the Loose WI did not think it was funny at all. They pointed out that the correct pronunciation was Looz, which seemed to me even worse, but it was all smoothed out eventually and I was even invited to speak in their area, so it shows how forgiving WIS can be. I mentioned the Loose Women's Institute a little later at a WI meeting in Morecambe, and it was received in stony silence. Only afterwards did I discover that just outside Morecambe there is an Institute at a village called Bare, and they do not laugh at that kind of joke any more.

There is a substantial difference between these gatherings and the ladies' luncheon clubs on which the lecture agencies largely rely for their regular business. They have professional speakers at most of their meetings, generally every member knows precisely what they are being paid, and they expect, quite rightly, a professional standard. One agency even arranges a private view of its speakers, when club secretaries can cross-examine them, weigh up their charms, and for all I know even feel their muscles and count their teeth. Thank goodness, the clubs I visit are prepared to take me on trust.

Ladies' Circlers, the wives of Round Tablers, are different again. Being by definition mostly in their twenties and thirties (Tablers are 'axed' when they are forty) they make a delightful audience which any red-blooded male can hardly fail to enjoy. Tablers themselves can be a much tougher proposition. They are not inclined to suffer poor speakers gladly, particularly those who assume that because their listeners have a few pints inside them all they want is a stream of smutty jokes. Sometimes, I must admit, it is not surprising that this is the impression they give. The days of hurling sugar lumps and bread rolls (and, on one gruesome occasion I recall, lemon meringue pie) are I hope long since over. Sometimes a boisterous evening is allowed to deteriorate into hooliganism, and then small wonder if the visiting speaker treats his audience accordingly, but on the whole Tablers are a discerning lot, even in their cups, and a speaker generally gets the reception he deserves.

This is not always the case at Rotary meetings, which have the built-in disadvantage of taking place at lunchtime. With the best will in the world, Rotarians who have businesses to run or jobs to keep cannot always linger after lunch to give the speaker a fair hearing. If the service has been slow and the president has allowed the business agenda to drag on, it can be 2.15 when the speaker rises, and the exodus will begin around 2.30. If the coffee cups are rattling and the washers-up are clattering and chattering in the kitchen, this can add up to a very hard-earned fee, but these are hazards one must expect to encounter, and indeed one is paid to do so. They are far outweighed by the excitement of facing a strange audience, of being entirely dependent on one's own ability to hold that audience for the next half-hour or more while they sit on uncomfortable chairs in a draughty hall after an indigestible meal, longing for the bar or the loo. I enjoy it enormously. It is after all the nearest I shall get to that revolving stage at the London Palladium.

Bob of course thought me quite mad. He always refused such invitations, though no one would be better able to hold a hall

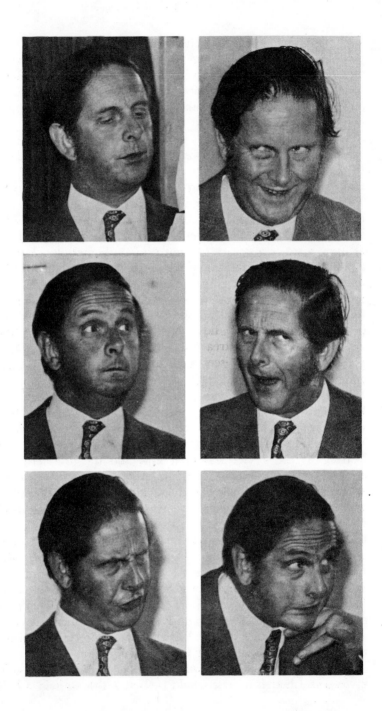

enthralled. Personally I could see little distinction professionally between addressing six hundred insurance men in the Norwood Rooms in Norwich and addressing six million viewers from the Television Centre in Shepherd's Bush, but Bob would as soon have gone round telling fortunes from tea-leaves or juggling with Indian clubs.

There was, however, one spare-time interest we shared for a while, rather to the astonishment of us both. We became part-owners, with ten others, of the 'Today' horse. It was a small syndicate with small resources, and we could only buy a small horse. 'If it fails as a racehorse,' we used to say. 'we could always enter it in the Greyhound Derby.' It also had the unfortunate habit of biting the stable door and refusing to release it and on occasions there were fears that it would actually appear on the track with the door still clamped between its teeth, but it confounded us all by actually winning one race and being placed in another and at least this reduced our losses to manageable proportions.

Its name was officially registered as Today, and it ran in specially devised breakfast-time colours of burnt-toast brown and marmalade orange, with a tomato-juice cap. It cost us only eight hundred guineas, which is peanuts in the racing world, but on its first outing of the 1974 season it came fourth, on its second it was only just behind the winner (with Bob and me doing an hysterical live commentary in the sports news), and the third time out it won the two o'clock at Epsom. It so happened that this triumph coincided with the presentation of the Radio Programme of the Year award to the 'Today' team for the third successive year, and most of us were attending the congratulatory luncheon at the Connaught Rooms. I sneaked out before the coffee to call our tame bookie and to listen to his track commentary; it was a photo finish and I had to fend off an infuriated queue while the judges made up their minds, but I gather my re-entry into the dining room was a sight to behold. I had won only a couple of pounds, but to own even one fetlock of a winning racehorse was glory enough.

'Then there was the morning we said it was 7.30 when it was actually half past eight, and the whole nation ground to a standstill'. Not a funny-face competition but a genuine sequence of the after-dinner speaker in full cry. Television newsreading was never quite like this. [*Middlesex Advertiser and Gazette*]

Today with two of his twelve owners. In the 'Today' colours of burnt toast and marmalade with tomato-juice cap he actually won one of his races, but the prize money hardly covered his breakfasts. [BBC *Copyright*]

After that, the only way our horse could go was down. The unfortunate beast jolted itself in some fashion and developed an allergy to running round corners. If the course curved, Today went straight on. It also seemed to lose interest after four furlongs, which is pretty disastrous in a five-furlong race. I watched him once more up in Doncaster, when he failed hopelessly to get in the frame (as we racing buffs used to say). Soon afterwards the little chap was sold to some speculator in Singapore to race on the local tracks there, and bearing in mind that Singapore is quite small and that Today still disliked turning corners, he probably finished up in the sea, poor thing. It was all a bit of a chuckle while it lasted, but it must have cost us about ten pounds a titter, and it confirmed what every racing man knows: that there is only one quicker way of losing money than betting on horses and that is to own one.

By the time we retired from the racing world, however, our

140

syndicate had already been disbanded. Marshall Stewart, editor of 'Today' since its general overhaul, left us to run the newly formed Independent Radio News, taking with him Douglas Cameron as his star newsreader and early-morning linkman, and one or two other members of the 'Today' team. Bob himself, with 'Brain of Britain' added to his other commitments, 'The Book Programme' about to start on television, a technical series on statistics lined up and the promise of a new weekly series on radio called 'Stop the Week', decided to call it a day with 'Today'. 'I am becoming a zombie,' he told the Press. 'I want to enjoy a decent night's sleep again.' We had a spectacular farewell breakfast of kedgeree, strawberries and champagne. As well as the usual presentations I gave Bob as a memento the earpiece he had used each morning during those three years – the 'appliance' that he always requested when he lost it in the office, to the embarrassment of new secretaries. We exchanged good wishes, bade each other goodbye, and I went back to the studio to speculate on who would sit in that empty chair beside me tomorrow.

Chapter Fifteen

It turned out to be not any one person in the other presenter's chair but a procession. The new editor, Alastair Osborne, deputy to Marshall for the previous four years, announced that we were not looking for one individual to replace Bob. We would be relying instead on what one newspaper described as 'a team of rotating announcers', which took me back to the old Magic Roundabout days on the Victoria Memorial. Whether this was deliberate policy, or was merely because no individual could be found to make that 4.30 rise every morning, I have never really established, but it meant that for some time the presentation of 'Today' was not so much a duet as a square-dance: 'Change your partner, rotate around . . .'

During Marshall's regime prospective presenters had been tried out in the comparative privacy of the Saturday morning programme, which was briefer, quieter and lighter than the weekday editions. They had ranged from the Atlantic rower, John Ridgway, who I assume decided that his Adventure School offered less hardships than our breakfast-time battle with the opt-outs, to the enchanting Mary Marquis, who very reasonably must have decided against commuting daily between Edinburgh and Portland Place. After Robert's departure the auditions were staged rather more publicly, and a succession of figures, familiar and unfamiliar, appeared in the co-presenter's chair every morning.

Mike Clayton, a former reporting colleague in Television News and now editor of *Horse and Hound*, was one of the earliest. He had been a relief presenter in Bob's day, and stayed on as a 'rotater'. Nancy Wise, a veteran of 'The World at One' and 'Pick of the Week', joined us briefly, then concentrated on 'You and Yours'. James Burke, whom I first met when he and Raymond Baxter came on the programme to publicise 'Tomorrow's World' – I gather I infuriated Raymond by introducing them as 'the technological Morecambe and Wise' – made a number of appearances for us but found it difficult to fit us in with his television travels. Alan Watson from 'Panorama' and 'The Money Programme' paid us a few visits, then found himself an EEC post in Brussels. Alan Coren of *Punch* was approached but decided against it. Melvyn Bragg, once described to me as Robert Robinson in paperback, came and rapidly went. It reached the stage, as I plodded into the office from Monday to Friday, when it would not have surprised me if I found one of the commissionaires, or some passing cabbie, occupying the adjoining chair.

Bob had left in June, and by the end of the summer the gaps were beginning to show. The *Sunday People* wrote: 'Mornings just haven't been the same since the witty, fast-talking, oh-so-clever Robert Robinson left "Today".' A correspondent in the *Radio Times* implored: 'Start the hunt for another Robinson to produce that magical catalytical relationship that has kept us alert in the mornings.' It was just the kind of comparison we had tried to avoid, since the idea had not been to find another Robinson, just as we had not wanted another de Manio three years before. Alastair fought back gamely: 'August is always a problem on any daily programme,' he wrote. 'Broadcasters, like the rest of the population, are entitled to take a summer holiday. Some programmes get around this by closing down for a month or two. Not so "Today".'

So 1974 proved to be a long, sticky summer, but finally a pattern emerged from our tangled skein of presenters. Desmond Lynam of the sports department, an able 'relief' presenter from Bob's day, joined me on a regular basis for the first half of the week, and Barry Norman, presenter of 'Film 74' and in due course of its successors 'Film 75' and 'Film 76', came in for the second half, including a solo run on Saturdays. Heather Summerfield – 'Heather the Weather' – took over Douglas Cameron's spot, the faithful Malcolm Billings was available for emergencies, and with the help of our new deputy editor Colin Adams we took the programme on the road again for prestige occasions like the American mid-term elections and the Dublin EEC Summit. We were beginning to look something like a team again.

Throughout all these changes one feature of 'Today' survived. It was introduced in Bob's time as a useful way of filling those awkward twenty seconds before the weather forecast or after the review of the papers, and it served us well for three years or more until our masters decreed that it had had its day. At its peak it was attracting up to a hundred letters a week, and even after it was dropped from the programme its supporters continued, to this day, to write in. It became known to millions as the 'Today' ho-ho.

It started quite accidentally, with one of us quoting an amusing misprint or an ambiguous headline. You can find the same sort of thing in many newspaper columns, whether it is Peterborough in the *Telegraph* or Men and Matters in the *Financial Times*, but the spoken word gives it an extra dimension. The more we quoted, the more were sent in; many were duplicates, some were unrepeatable, others I vowed to save for my last morning on the programme (and I have them still). There could be no doubt, from the volume of post we received, that the listeners delighted in these literary banana-skins, on which the most dignified and portentous of passages could be up-ended.

In their simplest form they would be just an incorrect letter, or a figure misplaced. Thus you would find bargain offers costing more than the price they had been reduced from, and notices of forthcoming events to be held last year, or a car with thirty miles on the clock and twenty-two owners. Houses would be advertised with 'bad rooms' and 'loving rooms' and extensive gardens, 100 feet by 20 inches. Sometimes a complete line was dropped, so that we found advertised in the *Wirral Globe*, for instance, 'a luxury six-berth internal flush toilet, with running water, ideal for fishing, swimming and sailing.'

To me the real delights were the ambiguities and the unlikely juxtapositions. I suspect it was not entirely accidental, for instance, that a *Financial Times* sub-editor, under the big heading 'Insulation', added as the sub-head 'UK Lags Behind'. I wonder, though, who let through the list of television programmes in the *Sunday Mirror* which contained one item called 'Keep Your Nose Clean', followed immediately by the instruction, 'See Pick of the Week'.

Some headlines, of course, are ambiguous enough on their own. Readers of the *Evesham Journal*, for example, may have been startled by the announcement, 'Town endorses spraying of weedkiller on Ham', unless they knew that Ham was a conservancy area by the Severn; certainly the very serious trade magazine *Industrial Relations* seemed to be entering a whole new field with its headline, 'More contacts with small firm bodies in Europe'. The stories themselves can provide similar double entendres. In a court case about pollution reported in the *Cumberland and Westmoreland Herald* it was noted that 'dead fish in a river are to be replaced by three farmers'. Also on the theme of conservation, a letter in the *West Briton* exhorted: 'During the Festival of Britain we had a slogan, take your litter home with you; it is not too late to bring it back again.' The *Daily Telegraph* gets my special award for an article about a distinguished lady magistrate: 'Fifteen years as a magistrate, at Bow Street dealing with prostitutes and at Great Marlborough Street – mainly shoplifting from the big stores – have brought her a wardrobe of plain navy and black dresses suitable for the Bench.'

We received a great many of these contributions from Ireland. The Irish are avid followers of the BBC, and build enormous aerials on their roofs so that they can pick up a free feed of BBC programmes and then complain about their low standard. The 'Today' programme attracted a wide audience north and south of the border in spite of their own indigenous entertainment, and I always found it heartening, at times of particular unpleasantness in the province or along the border, to receive a cutting from the *Belfast Telegraph* or the *Irish Times* with a comment like 'We can still enjoy a ho-ho'. Some of these Irish ones were so delightful that I could never decide whether they were intentional, accidental or just plain Irish. How about this, for instance, from the 'Advice to Readers' in the *Dublin Evening Press*. A reader asked if it was safe to eat the cockles from the local beach and the reply was: 'Shellfish from some areas are risky at the best of times. So be on the safe side, and leave them for the visitors.' There was one Irish ho-ho, incidentally, I never dared to use, even though an Irishman sent it in. It was the wrapping from a pound of sausages which bore the inscription, 'Eight thick sausages – Irish recipe'.

Sausage wrappings were quite an average part of the ho-ho post. It ranged from imported food packets with eccentric recipes, like 'Take the pancakes and lie down in the frying-pan', to an order of service from a wedding in Devon which advised the congregation that 'During the signing of the register, Sheep May Safely Graze'. There was a constant flow of church magazines and society newsletters with notices like 'Garden Plants Bring-and-Buy Sale – No Clothes Please', or an appeal for a summer

145

January Council

More contacts with small firm bodies in Europe

One man's misprint is another man's ho-ho; some of the printing eccentricities which were used to leaven the more serious news of the day.

fair which ended 'We know you will all get busy turning out your drawers for white elephants'. The Post Office has co-operated nobly on occasions with the little homilies it includes in its postmarks. At one time we had a spate of Inland Revenue demands passed on to us which bore on the envelope the helpful advice: 'Distress? Despair? Ring the Samaritans'; and a man in Manchester received the notification of the date of his driving test with the message franked on it, 'Get there by bus, leave the driving to us'. The poor chap failed, and no wonder.

From all this welter of 'Crash Courses for Learner Drivers', and 'Lost, one goshawk with bells – if found, please ring', and 'McQueen is only 2, and the more mature yesterday were trying to remember if there had ever been a younger captain of the Scottish team', one or two stand out as particularly memorable ho-hos. Who could resist, for instance, the *Guardian* report of a pornography case which quoted Mrs Mary Whitehouse as saying: 'All those who are exploiting bona fide sex education to make porn and cash must see the red light'; and I was asked to pass on to Buckingham Palace a Moroccan tourist leaflet about the Royal Palace in Rabat which said: 'The Royal Guard stands watch at all the gateways, waiting to be relieved in a ceremony well worth seeing.' My all-time favourite is a headline which appeared over a cricket story in the *Telegraph* back in 1972. It said simply: 'At last Virgin (121) has share of the luck.'

These then were the ho-hos which helped us survive the hazards of the post-Robinson months and the gloom of the world around us. Thanks to the continuing efforts of the entire team, in the year in which Bob and Marshall left us we had the considerable satisfaction of winning once again, for the fourth time, the Radio Industries Club award for Radio Programme of the Year. It was presented in the following April, the month in which I celebrated my fifth anniversary with the programme. Since this fell on April Fools' Day, it was marked not only by some lively festivities in the 'Today' office but also by a couple of jolly japes on the programme itself. Major John Blashford-Snell, hero of many dramatic expeditions, from the Zaire to the Darien Gap, told us about a tribe up the Zampopo who worshipped the sacred pith helmet of Sanders of the River. Because of the enormous loads they carried, their heads were lower than their shoulders so they were unable to wear headgear themselves and marvelled at anyone who could. The major himself was therefore treated as a minor god, and accorded the sacred greeting handed down by Sanders, 'Pith off'. In the same programme, and this even had me fooled, we interviewed a bird-lover who was planning to tow an island in the Medway out of the path of shipping, to preserve the nesting-place of the rare black-headed gull. It was all in the tradition of Richard Dimbleby's spaghetti-forests, and afforded us a little harmless fun.

However, the summer of 1975 was to bring more problems. Because of a change in Barry's television commitments, Desmond's extra duties as a boxing commentator and the usual holiday hazards, our regular pattern of presenting had to be broken. The ho-hos came under attack, perhaps because we were relying too heavily on them in the absence of other light relief, and were eventually dropped. What used to be praised as 'healthy cynicism' was now condemned as 'trivialisation'. Indeed, as Val Arnold-Foster wrote in the *Guardian*, 'Triviality is the fashionable complaint to make about "Today",' and the fashionable critics duly made it, from *The Listener* to *The Times*. It was perhaps significant that throughout this period the Audience Research Department continued to record as high an 'appreciation index' as ever – the ordinary listener was not apparently paying as much attention to *The Listener* and *The Times* as he should. Certainly on my travels around the luncheon clubs and the annual dinners the reaction to the programme was as enthusiastic as ever, but in the higher echelons within Broadcasting House, some disquiet was being expressed about its presentation.

It is difficult to detect when precisely we got back on course. It may have been during the party conferences, when Colin Adams led our team in Blackpool and organised the most comprehensive coverage in the programme's history. For those who mock the number of BBC staff at these conferences (it is said that we could probably outvote the delegates) it is worth recording that the three of us from 'Today', deputy editor, producer and presenter, turned out an average of seven items per programme on each morning of the conference, which makes nearly two hours of broadcasting a week. They included an interview with the Prime Minister which was widely quoted in the Press, and the only interview with Mrs Thatcher on any programme throughout the Conservative conference. *The Times* Diary continued to jeer, but only, one suspected, because of a dearth of any new ideas. *The*

Listener was now frequently quoting observations and interviews from a programme that its critic had once labelled 'trivial'.

However no matter how good our 'guest presenters' might be, it was now accepted that listeners liked continuity, voices they were used to, personalities which did not change from day to day. The idea of 'rotating announcers' was finally dropped, and in November there came the major turning-point, when Alastair found a presenter who was prepared to give priority to 'Today' over his other commitments, at least for three days a week. Brian Redhead, newly resigned from the editorship of the *Manchester Evening News*, an experienced journalist and broadcaster who had served a spell in television and decided on radio as the more satisfying medium, brought to us the stability the presentation

The 1976 'Today' team. Brian Redhead, Northumbrian-born and former editor of the *Manchester Evening News*, brought added northern appeal to the programme. 'Today' now linked Manchester and London, and the presenters linked Chorleywood and Cheadle Hulme. [BBC *Copyright*]

badly needed. As 1975 ended, another new 'Today' era began.

It so happened that at about this time, as part of the general BBC policy of interchanging the sequence editors, Alastair Osborne moved to the evening sequence, to edit 'Newsdesk' and

'The World Tonight', and his successor was Mike Chaney, former newspaperman, a senior producer on 'Today' for many years, and founder-editor of the snappy 'Newsbeat' programme on Radio 1. He is a man of considerable enthusiasm in many fields, and the BBC handout announcing his appointment drew attention to one of them: he and his wife, between them and from previous marriages, have produced twelve children, a revelation which prompted one paper to observe that 'surely a late-night appointment would have been more in the public interest.'

The changes soon started. In the first month reporters were despatched around the United Kingdom to present substantial reports from Belfast on Northern Ireland politics, from Coventry on Chryslers, from Birmingham on the new exhibition ground; and I presented one programme from Heathrow to mark the inaugural flight of Concorde. In the second month there was an experimental week when Brian presented half the programme from Manchester while I remained in London, a devolutionary device which not merely added a northern flavour to what had always been a southern-based programme, but also enabled Brian, living in Cheadle Hulme, to present on five mornings instead of three. It proved so successful that in April the London–Manchester presentation was introduced on a permanent basis, a revolutionary move in British current affairs broadcasting, Studio guests were invited to remain after their own interview was over, to comment on the topics which followed; the timings of the sports news, the review of the papers and the news summaries were juggled about with unprecedented freedom to fit in with the major items. Daily commentaries were circulated in the office on the quality of each programme, and generally life took on a whole new unexpectedness.

Whatever changes are taking place in the structure of 'Today', its essential character will I hope be retained, and with it the very special relationship which has been built up over the years between those who have regularly presented it and the three groups who are essential to its success; not only my many good friends in the production team, but those other two groups, the people who take part and the people who listen.

There is a book to be written one day about the characters who have appeared on the 'Today' programme since it was launched in 1957. In the 'Today' office there is an index in which the details of every contributor are filed, under various general headings, and there is one section for those who are impossible to classify. It is just headed 'People'; and under 'People' you will find the cream of the 'Today' eccentrics. The entries speak for themselves: 'Leicestershire Woman is Whistling Wonder' . . . 'Man who catches Icebergs' . . . 'Postman sings Happy Birthday through Letterboxes' . . . 'Pedalling Butcher Crosses Channel' . . . 'Carlisle Man Claims to be World's Biggest Liar' . . . The section is packed with offbeat inventors, men who can run cars on chicken manure, or grow square tomatoes. The most ingenious was a gentleman from Tunbridge Wells, who claimed to have invented a noiseless alarm clock; a more macabre idea of his was a klaxon for corpses. It was a time when cases had occurred of 'deaths' being wrongly diagnosed and 'corpses' waking up in mortuaries. In case they woke up too late, he suggested that every coffin should have a long klaxon, with the bulb resting in the hand of the deceased and the other end emerging from the ground. The slightest twitch down below would produce a toot on the klaxon, and sharp-eared cemetery patrols would forthwith start digging. Somehow it never caught on.

If 'People' were not inventing, they were collecting. They ranged from the film fan who collected so many old film magazines that the floor sagged and the walls bulged and the neighbours got a court order to stop him, to the geologist who collected fossilised dinosaur footprints and kept the lumps of rock all round his garden. This prompted one of the finest pay-off lines of any 'Today' interview, from a lady who, on discovering what they were, observed: 'How remarkable they should come so close to the house!'

There have been men who ate light bulbs, men who ate live goldfish, one man who came into the studio and ate spiders out of a jam-jar – 'I like the little red ones, they're nice and juicy . . .' There was the man compiling a flea map of Britain, of special value, I remember observing, for itch-hikers; and the man who made a circuit of the country leapfrogging letterboxes, not for a bet or for charity, but because he just enjoyed jumping over letterboxes. More recently we had a recital from the musical RAF sergeant who played 'Rule Britannia' by hitting himself on the head with a nine-inch spanner.

In the studio itself we have had some delightful impromptu performances. There was the old gentleman who was about to go out after completing his interview, then unexpectedly returned to

151

the microphone, leaned over Bob Robinson's shoulder as he was introducing the next item, and asked the entire nation where he had left his hat. There were the two genial ladies whom I interviewed at the end of the programme, and when I closed it with the usual formula, 'A very good morning to you,' they both piped up, 'And good morning to you too, dearie'. The most memorable performer of all was Miss Barbara Cartland, whom I interviewed about honey. Fortunately the interview was pre-recorded, because in the middle of it Miss Cartland presented me with a bottle labelled Melbrosia for Men. 'What does it do?' I ingenuously enquired. By the time she had finished telling me, the producer decided that perhaps we had better not broadcast that part of the interview; but the studio managers kept the tape, and it was a great success at their next Christmas party.

Such are the 'People' who have passed through the 'Today' studio; long may they prosper. The last, most important group is of course the listeners to 'Today'. I may meet more of them than most broadcasters do, through talks and luncheon clubs and dinners. In 1975 alone my 'live' audiences totalled nine thousand, the majority of them regular 'Today' listeners, and I met personally as many of them as possible. Over the years many more have written to us and telephoned us and sent us greetings at Christmas, culminating in the astonishing reaction to that somewhat ill-conceived award from 'Woman's Hour', Male Chauvinist Pig of the Year. Never has an award based on such a tiny poll (I received nine votes) achieved such massive publicity, and never has one rebounded quite so devastatingly. Hundreds of infuriated 'Today' listeners sprang to my defence; what started as a rather tasteless joke finished up as a most heart-warming demonstration of goodwill from loyal friends whom I had never met.

So if there are bleak mornings when the news is dreary, the interviews go badly and the jokes misfire, it is often the knowledge of that friendly army of 'Today' listeners which makes it worth while to try again; bishops and butchers, vice-admirals and vicars, postmen and peers, a whole cross-section of the population. People like Polly Elwes, who wrote: 'I was sitting in a traffic jam surrounded by hatchet-faced commuters when you read out the headline about Local Student Hit in Bollard, and it was extraordinary to look around and see virtually everyone roaring with laughter'; or the young woman in hospital in Jersey with a terminal illness, who could no longer read the papers and thanked us not only for bringing the news, but for helping her still to smile; or the many, many others who just tell us that their day starts that much better with 'Today'.

It is this relationship which gives the programme its extra dimension; this is what makes it something more than just another current affairs magazine at a rather awkward hour of the day. By bringing a little geniality into its journalism, by being informal as well as informative, and by blending good reporting with good cheer, it has earned a certain affection among those who listen to it and, though they may not admit it, among those who work on it too. Certainly for me it has offered a special kind of challenge, and just as special a reward. So for all the enjoyment they have brought me, to all those listeners, to the contributors and guests, and on this occasion *to* the 'Today' team, a very good morning to you – today and tomorrow.

Index

Adams, Colin 143, 148
'After Seven' 130-1
Alexandra, HRH Princess 56, 73
Anne, HRH Princess 123
Arnold-Foster, Val 148
Aspel, Michael 44, 112
Attenborough, David 104
Australia, Royal Tour of 61-72
Austria, National Service in 13-16; State Visit to 94

Baker, Richard 44
Bakewell, Joan 114
Banda, Dr Hastings 84
Banks, Basil 5
Banks, Lord (Desmond) 4
Banks-Smith, Nancy 103
Baxter, Raymond 142
Bedford, Peter 40
Bell, Peter 14
Billings, Malcolm 112, 143
Black, Peter 102, 103, 104
Bland, Leslie 17
Blankers-Koen, Fanny 122
Blashford-Snell, Major John 147
Blubberhouses 120
Bottomley, Arthur 85
Bragg, Melvyn 143
Brooks, Bryn 131
Brooks, Don 29
Brown, Douglas 36

Brown, (Lord) George 87
Burke, James 142
Burns, John 36

Cameron, Douglas 40, 108, 111-12, 114-15, 120, 141, 143
Cartland, Barbara 152
Catlow, Bob 84
Chaney, Mike 150
Chorleywood 93, 114, 117
Churchill, Sir Winston 42
Clayton, Mike 142
Colley, Ray 36
Conferences, Party 123-5
Coren, Alan 143
Cousins, (Lord) Frank 124
Crawley, John 80
Croxley Green 61
Cyprus 93-4
Czechoslovakia 103

Dee, Simon 116
de Gaulle, President Charles 54
de Manio, Jack 74, 106, 107-11, 114-16, 118, 143
Dereham & Fakenham Times 19, 21, 25, 33, 44
Dereham Players 28, 30
Dimbleby, Richard 58, 133, 148
Dougall, Robert 44, 45

155

Eastern Daily Press 19, 33, 36
Egremont, Baron 44
Elizabeth, HM Queen 49, 54, 55, 57, 65, 66, 67, 68, 69, 70, 77, 78, 79, 80, 82
Elizabeth, HM Queen Mother 49, 56, 57, 60
Ellison, John 133
Elwes, Polly 152
Ennals, Maurice 40
Ethiopia, State Visit to 76–9
'Euroflits' 121–3

Fitt, Peter 33
Fletcher, Freddie 21
Foote, Bert 89
Forsyth, Freddie 83
Fowler, Eileen 112
Fox, Roland 36
Friend, Bob 40, 112
Frost, David 99

Gaitskell, Hugh 124
Gibraltar 89–92
Gloria 118
Goad, Gerry 87, 93
Goldie (the Golden Eagle) 82
Gomer-Jones, Ronnie 49
Greece 92–3
Griffiths, Mary 118
Griggs, Tony 84

Hardcastle, William 74, 102
Harley, Mervyn 5
Hennig, Frank 112
Hesketh, Bernard 75, 93, 94, 96
'Ho-hos' 143–7, 148
Hollowood, Bernard 102
Holmes, David 36
Hudson, Robert 74, 79, 80

Iceland, Prince Philip's visit to 75–6
Independent Radio News 141
'In Town Tonight' 133
Italy, State Visit to 57–8

Jackson, Anna 131
Jaffa, Max 123, 125
Johnston, Brian 74, 133
Jones, Christopher 35, 39

Kabaka of Buganda (King Freddie) 91, 92
Kaunda, President Kenneth 84, 88
Kendall, Kenneth 44
Kent, HRH Duke of 59
Kerrison, George and Molly 24

Ladies' Circle 137
Lalor, David 6
Lebanon, fighting in 94–7
Lee-Potter, Lynda 135
Lejeune, Anthony 4
Lidell, Alvar 39
'Life in the Nine' 131
Listener, The 42, 148, 149
Living Decisions 133–4
Longford, Lord 121
Luncheon Clubs 134, 136–7, 148, 152
Lunghi, Hugh 103
Luxembourg, EEC meeting in 113
Lynam, Desmond 110, 143, 148

MacColl, René 62, 78, 81, 82
Macmillan, Harold 47
Macpherson, Tony 89

Malta, State Visit to 93
Maltby, Tom 36–7, 39, 83
Manchester, recording in 131; presentation from 150
Margaret, HRH Princess 49, 55, 56
Marquis, Mary 142
Matthews, Freddie 56, 57
Matthews, Peter 92
McDermid, Angus 36
Merchant Taylors' School 1, 4, 60
Milner, Donald 36
Minson, Basil 14
Moore, Dr Barbara 48
Mulchrone, Vincent 62
Muncaster, Martin 74
Murray, Pete 132–3
Mycock, Bert 35

'Newsbeat' 150
'Newsdesk' 107, 149
'Newsroom' 99–104, 107
New York 123
New Zealand, Royal Tour of 61–72
Nickolls, Louis 49
Nicol, Bill 94, 96
Nkomo, Joshua 86
Norman, Barry 143, 148
North Elmham 22
Northern 'Gardeners' Question Time' 132
Northern Ireland 11–12, 34, 88–9, 123, 150
NUJ 117

'Object in Question, The' 132
Obote, Milton 91, 92
Ogilvy, Angus 73
'Open House' 132–3

Osborne, Alastair 142, 143, 149
'Out of the Rut' 131
Paisley, Rev. Ian 88–9
Paris, State Visit to 131
Parkin, Leonard 36
Parkinson, Michael 114, 116
Parrott, Mr 114
'People Ltd' 131
Philip, HRH Prince 49, 56, 61, 66, 70, 72, 75, 76
Phillips, Frank 39
'PM' 107
Powell, Mrs Margaret 134
Priestland, Gerald 36, 98

Radio Industries Club 125, 139, 147
'Radio Newsreel' 39, 42
Read, Ronnie 67
Redhead, Brian 149, 150
Reed, Freddie 67, 68
Reynolds, Gillian 114
Rhodesia, UDI in 84–8, 89–90
Ridgeway, John 142
Rippon, Geoffrey 113
Robins, Brian 6, 10, 16
Robinson, Robert 116, 117–23, 126, 128, 129, 132, 137, 139, 141, 143, 147, 152
Robson, Ronald 36
Rotary 137
Round Table 28, 30, 134, 136, 137
Russell, Audrey 55, 59

St John Stevas, Norman 117
Salmon, Douglas 132
Scase, Tony 132
Schumann, Maurice 113
Scott, Peter Hardiman 36

Sebastian 112
Sharpley, Anne 79, 81
Sicily, Mafia activities in 93
Simpson, John 36
Sithole, Ndabaningi 86
Smith, Douglas 131
Smith, Ian 84, 85, 89–90
Smith, Patrick 58
Snagge, John 39, 43
Soames, Sir Christopher 122
Standley, Diana 21
Stewart, Marshall 40, 106, 112–13, 116, 117, 118, 120, 121, 125, 141, 147
Streeter, Fred 112
Studd, Ted 87, 88, 91
Sudan, State Visit to 81–2
Summerfield, Heather 143

Talbot, Godfrey 35, 50, 54, 59, 60, 62
Tayar, Graham 134
'Ten O'Clock' 74, 123
Thatcher, Mrs Margaret 148
Thomas, Leslie 62
Thompson, Sir Herbert 32, 33
Thompson, Teddy 50
'Thought for the Day' 108, 110, 121, 128
Tidmarsh, John 36
'Tiger', HMS 89–90
Timpson, Jeremy 29, 61
Timpson, Joy 5
Timpson, Nicholas 61, 73
Timpson, Pat 17–19, 22, 24, 37, 61, 67, 93, 97, 126, 130
'Today' 2, 9, 43, 74, 105–29, 130, 131, 132, 133, 135, 136, 139, 141, 142–53
'Today', racehorse 139–40
'Town and Around' 44, 45

Townswomen's Guilds 134–6
Tunisia, Queen Mother's State Visit to 56–7
Turnbull, Alec 40
Turnill, Reginald 35
'Twenty Questions' 133

Uganda, fighting in 91–2

Voss-Bark, Conrad 36

Watson, Alan 143
Wembley News 5–10, 16, 37
'What's It All About? 133
Wheatley, Alan 34, 35
Whitby, Tony, 125
White, Fraser 133
Whiting, Gerald 6, 10, 16
Whitmore, Richard 135
Williams, Mrs Shirley 117
Wilson, (Sir) Harold 84, 89–90, 148
Windfall Cottage 24
Wise, Nancy 142
'Woman's Hour' 152
Women's Institutes 134–6
Woodall, Corbet 53
Woods, Maurice 21, 28–9
Woods, Peter 83, 102
Woon, Peter 83, 98, 102, 103, 104, 107, 115
'World at One, The' 74, 98, 107, 115, 142
'World Tonight, The' 107, 150
Worsley, Katherine (Duchess of Kent) 59

Young, Capt. M. 16

Zambia, after UDI 84–8